The Sins of Sickness
An Alcoholic Believer's Perspective

By Mark Evenson

Copyright © 2008 by Mark Evenson. All Rights Reserved.
Editor, Heather E. Hershey. Self published at lulu.com.
ISBN: 978-0-578-01362-6
NASB Version used for all Biblical references.

Dedicated to the memory of my mother—the very lifeblood of our family: Dad and your three boys sure do miss you.

DEDICATIONS

I dedicate this book to my father, my two children, Matthew and Jennie, and their mother. When my drinking had reached the chronic stage, and most of my family and friends had sought higher ground, they indeed held firm. They had to witness and endure the horror show the longest, and still persevered. As a father and a son, I have been fortunate. When it comes to support, I may not have had quantity, but I certainly have had quality. They will never know what they have meant to me. They just will never know.

To my special friends who really tried to help: Curly K., Tim S. Graig L., and yes, Tim O.

In memory of Heather Knoll and her mother, Robin Bucholz. Robin, if Heather had your inner strength and compassion, then Heaven's gain was truly the world's loss. Thanks much for all your help.

Last, but certainly not least, Donald Root, who I thank with all the gratitude I can muster. He has been my pastor, my spiritual adviser, my partner and confidant, and most of all, my friend. Anyone who gets to deal with Don comes away a better person for it. His time and effort to help put this book together will never be forgotten. I will remember him even more for the decency of his life. There are very few human beings in this world I could ever really say I admired, but Don would be one of them. I cannot emphasize enough what he has meant to my life and the completion of this book.

Forward By Pastor Donald Root

In the early Summer of 2006, as I played golf at a course on the grounds of the local VA Hospital, I began to regularly catch up with three men who would always invite me to join their group. Within a few weeks, we began to make plans to meet at a specified time and play the entire round together. Over the ensuing weeks, I began to really hit it off with one of the men, by the name of Mark Evenson. I learned that he was a resident at the local VA Hospital, enrolled in one of their alcohol rehab programs. On several occasions we had the opportunity to play a round with just the two of us, and our discussions began to move toward the realm of the spiritual. Mark informed me that he had written a book while in jail. I asked if I could read it, and the next evening he handed me the original manuscript.

I don't know what I was expecting, but late that evening as I began to make my way through what he had written, I was completely taken aback at what he had to say. I couldn't put it down. I re-read much of it several times. I read large sections to my wife. The second night, I stayed up way past midnight to scan the entire manuscript onto my computer. After two days, I handed it back to Mark, and he asked for my reaction. I told him that he was very close to believing exactly as I do. We laughed together because we had developed a good-natured rivalry over our respective denominational differences.

Since that day, over two years ago, I have watched Mark battle to apply the principles he communicates in this book, because I have had a front row seat. I have seen him fail and battle his way back. Life is rarely easy for any of us, and rebuilding a life from the ravages of alcoholism has to rate up there with one of the toughest of roads. I have seen him suffer when he has failed to yield to the Spirit, and I have seen him cling tenaciously (and desperately) to Christ at some of his darkest hours. I have seen God do some truly miraculous things for Mark just when he needed it most—to show him that He really cares for him personally. I have seen God actively work in his life to teach him what the Spirit-filled life is really all about. Most of all, I have seen Mark grow in his relationship with the Lord. He has been tested by fire and has learned to live these principles by faith and faith alone.

I know the heartbeat of why Mark wrote this book and what he hopes it will do for you because I have heard him expound on it many, many times. This is not a normal book. It was not written by a normal person or under normal circumstances. It does not have a normal message, so I do not believe it will have a normal impact. Read and consider what Mark has to say to you. You will be the better for it.

Donald Root (An Assistant Pastor)

Forward From the Author

This is the last addition to this book, and it is being written after everything you are about to read. I want you to know, that I have relapsed and went back to active drinking since I completed this book. What does this say about what I have written? What does this say about me? I want the reader to understand that I did not write this book after I had been sober a number of years like almost everyone else has done. I wrote this book while I was in the middle of a two year drunken stage and sitting in jail. I do not think that concept has ever been approached before. The truths in the book are even more applicable to people who are caught up in active drinking or considering relapse. DO NOT wait to deal with God until after you're clean and sober; because if you do, you may never find him. Everything I have written in this book is as true today as it was when I first wrote it.

Then what happened to me? I could not personally grasp three concepts I knew to be true, but simply could not accept. The first concept was whether I could genuinely take Jesus Christ at his word. I faced questions such as: Could He help remove the obsession? Would He truly give me life, and give it to me abundantly? Could He be trusted? There were times I did not trust Jesus at all. I have since discovered He indeed can be trusted, and that His word is good. He did for me what no human being or group of human beings could have ever done. I asked him and he delivered. Yes, He is good to His word.

Secondly, I questioned whether God was big enough, powerful enough, and truly able to help me get my life back. I wondered if He was able to do for me what I possibly could not do for myself. I found out, without a shadow of a doubt, yes. He is able to do and orchestrate any situation, any problem, any calamity that comes your way; and I truly believe He enjoys helping us when we are able to recognize and appreciate His love. That was the point where I failed. I had so little gratitude before, but I have a body full of it now. That was a hard lesson to learn.

Lastly, this is the most important point for you, for me, or anyone—I had to realize whether Christ cared enough about me personally to help and teach me to live again with happiness and a sense of peace. I am not talking about other Christians, the church, or anyone else. I am talking about me. I questioned if He cared enough about Mark Eddie Evenson, and me alone. I wondered if His love for me was that personal? As it turned out, it was. How I missed that idea I will never know, but I did. When there was no other way, no other people to help, He came to me alone. It simply does not get any better than that.

I grappled with God when I was in a state of active drinking and I am very lucky I did. If I had not, sobriety most likely would never have found me. If you are still drinking, read and contemplate what I have written anyway. Do not wait to get sober and find God, find him now. People do not get sober, then go to AA; they go to AA, then get sober. Similarly, people do not get their sins forgiven and then go to church. They go to church and find forgiveness. I always tell people don't wait to clean up your act and then go to church—go to church, and over time, the rest will come naturally. The same premise applies to AA. Don't wait to get sober and then go to AA—go now, and sobriety just might find you. My hope for you is that it does.

Mark Evenson

Introduction

Why This Book

I am writing this from the Rock County Jail, F-West Unit. Suffice to say, I have been at the top and at the bottom of life. This book is based on my own struggle with alcoholism—and mine alone. I have read *The Bible*, *The Big Book of A.A.* (Alcoholics Anonymous), as well as many other books and articles on the topics of: alcoholism, God, and the church. I have attended both church services and A.A. meetings. That being said, I think this book will be different from other books or messages you may have encountered in many respects. My goal is to attempt to connect with five types of people: the Christian alcoholic; the Christian nonalcoholic; the sober, recovering alcoholic who may not be a believer; and the family members and friends of the alcoholic.

There are a lot of questions that often are left unanswered or unaddressed regarding alcohol and Christianity. Some people may believe that being a Christian and an alcoholic may be a contradiction—but is it really? Is it possible to be involved in an active addiction and still be a believer? Many people often wonder what this struggle may entail. Some people even ask if it is possible to lose sobriety and still be in the family of God. *The Bible* has provided clear answers to these questions, and I can corroborate those truths through my own experience. Does that mean the Christian believer will avoid the consequences and the misery that comes with active drinking? That answer is a resounding, "NO!" In fact, if a person claims to be a Christian, those consequences will actually be worse. Scriptures tell us in II Peter 2:20-22:

> *(20) For if, after they have escaped the defilements of the world by the knowledge of the Lord and Savior Jesus Christ, they are again entangled in them and are overcome, the last state has become worse for them than the first. (21) For it would be better for them not to have known the way of righteousness, than having known it, to turn away from the holy commandment handed on to them. (22) It has happened to them according to the true proverb,* "A DOG RETURNS TO ITS OWN VOMIT,' *and,* 'A sow, after washing, returns to wallowing in the mire.'

Some people who read this book may think this author is nothing but a man trying to rationalize his behavior and actions—perhaps to some degree they are correct. I will let you make up your own mind about that question; however, I only ask that you read and contemplate this text carefully, reflecting not only on what I tell you, but what the Scriptures reveal. See how much of this information hits home.

One question often asked is whether a person who has been sober for many years, has never relapsed, been a decent person, and has been an active member of A.A., can still be at risk of eternal damnation of a literal Hell? *The Bible* tells us we can be certain of that fact. I give you this warning in love, not to be intolerant of this view. Jesus told us clearly in John 14:6: *"...I am the way, and the truth, and the life; no one comes to the Father but through Me."*

Salvation and sobriety complement each other well, but one idea does not necessarily guarantee the other. It is important for you to understand that point. If you know that if you died today you would be with Christ in Heaven, and He alone is that reason, good for you! You have already made the most important decision. You can have assurance of that fact, as we read in I John 5:11-12: *"(11) And the testimony is this, that God has given us eternal life, and this life is in His Son. (12) He who has the Son has the life; he who does not have the Son of God does not have the life."* If you have no relationship with Jesus Christ, I ask that you read on and think about what I have to say. Don't just ignore it though.

I will also touch on a sensitive subject people seem to avoid and know very little about—the taking of one's own life—suicide. Why? In the final stages of addiction, that action is always a possibility. Unfortunately, history bears that out. Some people will disagree with what I say. Others may be confused, and some people may be comforted. Again, I ask you to read on and decide, and more importantly, see what *The Bible* says on this topic. You may be surprised.

In closing, I will be as open and honest as I can with you. I believe there are many misconceptions today with what a Christian alcoholic faces and wrestles. The struggle is different for the unbeliever. Their life is just as painful, but they probably have not experienced the same types of regret.

Chapter 1

Alcoholism-What It Really Is

The medical profession has pronounced alcoholism to be a disease. According to the Big Book of Alcoholics Anonymous, alcoholism is a sickness of one's physical, emotional and spiritual being. *The Bible* declares alcoholism a sin. I call alcoholism a plague—a destructive, and at times, an out-of-control, all-encompassing plague. Webster's dictionary defines a plague as a "deadly epidemic disease." It is certainly all of that.

This plague reaches into every aspect of a person's life and is capable of destroying everyone in its path. I believe alcoholism can be evil in its rawest form. It has already destroyed individuals and families and killed millions more. The financial expense alcoholism has placed on society is enormous, and has placed the entire population at risk. This plague causes our jails and prisons to overflow at the cost of human suffering, as well as a financial strain that in reality, cannot even be calculated.

No one is immune to alcoholism, no matter what their station in life. This destructive force can overtake anyone at any time. When an addict drinks, the alcohol changes them almost completely. Anyone who has lived with or has known an alcoholic can certainly attest to this fact. The drinking may start out sporadically; however, the alcoholic's drinking can easily be seen by others, yet very rarely by the alcoholic. If allowed to progress to its final stages, the effects of alcoholism are totally devastating to the alcoholic, as well as to anyone close to them. Billy Graham once said in a tract about alcoholism that "overall, it was the worst plague that has ever raged this earth." He further stated that "alcohol has destroyed more people, more families, cost society more grief, than any other plague ever to hit this planet." He was correct.

There is no one on the planet that has not been affected by alcoholism in one way or another—*no one*. Any person, who has known an alcoholic or had to deal with one, knows what I am talking about. The effects of the alcoholic's drinking are heartbreaking not only for the alcoholic, but also for the people who love and care about them. At times, those devastating effects are almost impossible to watch, and can be so gut-wrenching.

I will not give you the reader, my "drunkalogue." My story is the same as others—fights, divorce, missed work, missed opportunities, people let down, irresponsibility, almost evil behavior at times—all when drinking. When I was not drinking, these types of problems did not dominate my life. I am not saying that I or my life was perfect, but that it was manageable. When I was drinking, my life was not so manageable. My wife Cathie, used to say there was Mark, and there was Al (her name for me when I drank), and neither she nor anyone else liked Al very much; and looking back now, I did not either.

One of the devastating effects of this disease is a form of complete amnesia regarding one's alcoholism. No matter how much the alcoholic may have suffered from their drinking, over time, and without constant reinforcement, they will seem to forget the horror they may have inflicted on themselves and others. At times, previous incidents will not even *enter* their minds. You may ask incredulously if that is really possible. Unfortunately it is. I am not trying to make excuses here, yet the alcoholic mind can be very untrustworthy and unreliable at critical times. The good news is that this condition can be avoided, but only when the alcoholic realizes they need help outside their own ability.

Many people may wonder if all alcoholics are the same and effected in the same way. For the most part they are, but the degrees of intensity may vary. Some cases of the disease may be mild, while others may experience more severe effects, just like someone might who had a cold, cancer, influenza or any other sickness or disease. In A.A., one is told some people are sicker than others, and this is a true statement. Some people may need two aspirin while others may need twenty-two. The effects of alcoholism work in the same way. As we go along through this book, I will talk more about alcoholism and its effects; but for now, I think you get the idea.

Lastly, you may wonder what the *Bible* says about the subject of alcohol. The *Bible* says the abuse of alcohol is sin, and that abuse will eventually rob you of everything you have. According to Proverbs 23:21, *"For the heavy drinker and the glutton will come to poverty, and drowsiness will clothe one with rags."* In fact, the *Bible* accurately portrays what life for an alcoholic is like in Proverbs 23:29-35:

> *(29) Who has woe? Who has sorrow? Who has contentions? Who has complaining? Who has wounds without cause? Who has redness of eyes? (30) Those who linger long over wine, those who go to taste mixed wine. (31) Do not look on the wine when it is red, when it sparkles in the cup, when it goes down smoothly; (32) at the last it bites like a serpent and stings like a viper.*

> *(33) Your eyes will see strange things and your mind will utter perverse things. (34) And you will be like one who lies down in the middle of the sea, or like one who lies down on the top of a mast. (35) 'They struck me, but I did not become ill; they beat me, but I did not know it When shall I awake? I will seek another drink.'*

There it is—everything but the alcoholic's phone number. After knowing and going through all of that, the alcoholic will still seek another drink, which is that amnesia factor. Why? Because at that point in their addiction, it is all they know, and the alcoholic will just deal with their disease the best way they can, and drinking is usually that way. God certainly does acknowledge alcoholism, but you may ask what His answer to all of this is. We will take a look at that answer in the next chapter of this book.

Now, what about the Christian *nonalcoholic*? The alcoholic battles addiction in much of the same way a nonalcoholic person may battle sin, and at times they will meet with similar results. As difficult as the alcoholic condition may be to understand or to relate, the next chapter should be helpful to you as well. The Christian nonalcoholic will discover ways they can even relate their own experiences to that of the alcoholic.

Chapter 2

What's Happening?

Have you ever asked yourself why you continue in your addiction? Perhaps you have asked why one would allow their self to go through such situations. Sick, shaky, ashamed, full of regret, remorse, and self-contempt—a Christian who has the Holy Spirit of God cannot avoid this state. Even though they are broken down and beat-up, they seem more than willing to do it all again. So what is happening here? This does not appear to be logical behavior. Trust me, at this point, the alcoholic has no more of a clue about what is happening to them than the people who have to watch them.

Let's look at a Biblical perspective. In these next few Scripture references, I will make several word substitutions for the sake of application, and to help you understand these verses in the context of addiction. I will replace the word "flesh" with "addiction," and I will replace the words "sin" and "law" with the words "first drink," since taking that first drink is breaking the law for the alcoholic.

> *Romans 7:14-25: For we know that the Law* (not taking that first drink) *is spiritual, but I am of flesh* (addiction), *sold into bondage to sin* (alcohol). *(15) For what I am doing, I do not understand; for I am not practicing what I would like to do, but I am doing the very thing I hate (16) But if I do the very thing I do not want to do, I agree with the Law, confessing that the Law is good. (17) So now, no longer am I the one doing it, but sin* (alcoholism) *which dwells in me. (18) For I know that nothing good dwells in me, that is, in my flesh* (addiction); *for the willing is present in me, but the doing of the good is not. (19) For the good that I want, I do not do, but I practice the very evil* (drinking) *that I do not want. (20) But if I am doing the very thing I do not want, I am no longer the one doing it, but sin* (alcoholism) *which dwells in me. (21) I find then the principle that evil is present in me, the one who wants to do good* (not drink). *(22) For I joyfully concur with the law of God in the inner man, (23) but I see a different law in the members of my body, waging war against the law of*

my mind and making me a prisoner of the law of sin (alcoholism) *which is in my members. (24) Wretched man that I am! Who will set me free from the body of this death? (25) Thanks be to God through Jesus Christ our Lord! So then, on the one hand I myself with my mind am serving the law of God, but on the other, with my flesh* (addiction) *the law of sin* (alcoholism). *Romans 8:1-2, Therefore there is now no condemnation for those who are in Christ Jesus. (2) For the law of the Spirit of life in Christ Jesus has set you free from the law of sin* (alcoholism) *and of death.*

Those verses vividly depict the alcoholic's struggle. Even when the alcoholic finally decides they really want to stop drinking, they soon discover they cannot. The alcoholic had always believed before that if they wanted badly enough, they simply could stop drinking. That is part of that denial stage. Now they have discovered that they cannot stop. You may ask what can one do now. The alcoholic has lost any control over the use of alcohol, and is more or less constantly drunk by this point. The trouble they have been experiencing with their spouse, their boss, the law, and within themselves, begins to tear the alcoholic apart. Usually, deep down, the alcoholic does not expect any one else to understand what is going on, since they do not have a clue to that state themselves. As *The Big Book* of A.A. says, "They are a baffled lot."

The next question someone will often ask about alcoholism is who or what can stop this vicious disease? The alcoholic's family cannot stop them from drinking; neither can their friends, boss or even their minister. The alcoholic can't stop their drinking. So who can help them, you may wonder. How bad does the alcoholic's condition have to get before they stop? The answers for the alcoholic are the same answers for every sinner—admit your sin and look outside yourself for help. The point of admitting the alcohol problem is difficult for most people, yet the alcoholic especially finds this step difficult. One's pride and desire to control one's own life is what makes this step difficult. Because of refusing to admit the alcohol problem and believing that one can control the problem if they simply try harder, that person will begin to make promises.

They might tell you the drinking or addiction will not happen again, or that they will try harder. Indeed, those promises will not turn out to be correct if they try to resolve the problems with their own limited abilities and strength. Their life will not be what it was like before. It will be worse. The only way an alcoholic can stop drinking, or that any one can stop their alcohol problem, is by completely living in the Spirit, and relying on the Spirit's control, rather than their own. Let me clarify an important point here; when I refer to the Spirit, I mean the Holy Spirit of the One, True Biblical God; not some energy or abstract higher power, or any other god. I am talking about Jesus Christ; and this is where many members of A.A. may bristle. Many A.A. members or leaders never want to even discuss a particular religion or sect, and I will discuss their reasoning for that choice later.

As with any sinner, the Holy Spirit teaches the alcoholic how to live in the strength of the Spirit by first admitting you are an alcoholic (sinner). Second, you need to ask for help, whether you choose clinical treatment, A.A., or whatever it takes. Third, you need to learn how to get and stay in the Spirit. You can learn how to stay sober. There is a way. The first two steps the alcoholic must do by themselves. The third step, God, along with others, must help and teach you so you will better be able to understand how critical it is for you to stay in the Spirit. I learned the hard way how important that last step was in my life.

It took the loss of everything—and I mean everything—in my life, to understand what it meant to live and stay in the Spirit. You don't have to get to that point, because even though the concept may sound simple, implementing the process can be very challenging. I was told how to live in the Spirit, but did not understand the value of that truth, because I thought I was smarter than most people. I later discovered that the truth of one being able to live in the Spirit was promised in verses such as John 14:26 which stated, *"But the Helper, the Holy Spirit, whom the Father will send in My name, He will teach you all things, and bring to your remembrance all that I said to you."* In order to claim that promise though, I would have to put myself in a physical location as well as a state of mind where the Holy Spirit could reach and teach me—and the tavern was not that place. What I am really talking about here is your environment. This is probably not a startling revelation to many people, but it is a point that is often overlooked.

Now we are led to the question about what type of environment should a person place themselves for the Holy Spirit to be most effective? Let me list a few examples for you: *The Bible*, A.A. meetings, the church, and *The Big Book* of A.A.—the Spirit of God permeates these sources. Through these environments He can communicate and teach you. Satan and the World do not control these environments; the Holy Spirit does.

Another important environment the Holy Spirit can work in is your prayer life. When you pray, Satan is defeated, lost, and out of the environment he can control. Now you will find the Spirit-filled life can be realized. You should still understand being in the right environment and striving to live a Spirit-filled life will not make you perfect. You still can choose to sin and make mistakes, but those sins will no longer dominate or destroy you. Instead, the Spirit-filled life begins to grow, and dominates your choices in life. Finally, good things will begin to happen in your life and most importantly, sobriety is a real possibility, rather than an unattainable goal. God promises us in Romans 8:28, *"And we know that God causes all things to work together for good to those who love God, to those who are called according to His purpose."*

To understand better the difference between a Spirit-controlled life and a life that is not under the control of the Spirit, we first need to understand we possess two natures. One nature is that of our flesh—our sinful, addictive nature; and the other is our Spirit-controlled nature. These two natures constantly war with each other, but never to a stalemate. One will win and dominate. Both natures lose battles, but only one wins the war. How do we know which nature will win the war? That is the nature you feed the most. If an alcoholic goes to the tavern, or the liquor store, or into the bottle, they will feed their addiction. They will become drunk. I am not anti-alcohol or anti-tavern for the normal drinker, but for the alcoholic, over time, these environments can be the kiss of death. I have been in many taverns for many, many hours, and I just never met sober, recovering people in them—never. There may be some who do go to these places, but I have never met or seen them personally. That is *why* these people are sober and recovering. Most of them understand the danger of being in those environments, so they do not expose their addictive nature to that temptation. Most of those sober and recovering alcoholics have learned this lesson the hard way. They do not fool around with their alcoholism any more, but give that disease the respectful distance it deserves, as any alcoholic should who wants to recover.

So far what I have written is fairly traditional thinking, except the excerpts from *The Scriptures* from the book of Romans. I hope the nonalcoholic Christian can relate to those Scriptures as well so they can better understand the alcoholic Christian's struggle. As I previously mentioned, that struggle is the same one the nonalcoholic has with sin. I am not trying to excuse the alcoholic's actions in any way, but just maybe this will help you understand the alcoholic does not want to fail either. If the alcoholic loses even one battle, the consequences are immediate and painful. Most sin is not that way.

In closing this chapter, I have been as precise as I can be without being too wordy. I have been careful about how I phrase some things, but that is about to change. At this point I have some bones to pick, so now it gets personal.

Chapter 3

The Church and A.A.

An alcoholic can often go to church, confess their sins, pray, even take communion, then leave, and by that same evening get drunk. Does this mean the church has failed the alcoholic or visa versa? Why do some Christian alcoholics fail to find sobriety, even when being loyal in attendance and commitment? This scenario happens a lot. Does that mean the church is blind to the alcoholic member? No, the church members are aware of the alcoholic's actions almost as much as the alcoholic's family and friends are aware. You are probably wondering why the church can't help that alcoholic stop drinking. Most often, the church is simply not equipped with the knowledge to address properly the disease of alcoholism. The people of the church usually care very much about that person and his struggle, and would do anything to help the alcoholic and their family, but do not know what to do. One of the best things they can do is to direct the alcoholic to Alcoholics Anonymous, what I believe is God's gift to alcoholics.

I honestly believe that God utilized Bill W. and Dr. Bob, the cofounders of Alcoholics Anonymous, as well as the rest of the early members of A.A., and created a way for alcoholics to find sobriety. I think the early members were inspired and driven by the Holy Spirit. God's Word even confirms this leading in John 16:13, *"But when He, the Spirit of truth, comes, He will guide you into all the truth; for He will not speak on His own initiative, but whatever He hears, He will speak; and He will disclose to you what is to come."*

I also believe what is written in *The Big Book* of A.A. is inspired by the Holy Spirit. For now, I want to emphasize that it is my solid belief that A.A. is a gift from Jesus Christ, and He with the assistance of A.A. is the Light the alcoholic needs to find. Christ told us in John 12:46, "I have come as Light into the world, so that everyone who believes in Me will not remain in darkness."

Everything I have read in *The Big Book* of A.A. has come directly or indirectly from *The Bible*. I have read both of these books several times, and *The Big Book* of A.A. is more or less the teachings of *The Bible* paraphrased. I will give you a prime example. Alcoholics Anonymous' famous and most quoted slogan is to live one's life "one day at a time."

Where did the writers of *The Big Book* of A.A. come up with that motto? I will quote what Jesus taught in Matthew 6:34, "*So do not worry about tomorrow; for tomorrow will care for itself. Each day has enough trouble of its own.*"

Dr. Bob, Bill W., and the early members of A.A. also started a tradition of saying the Lord's Prayer to close their meetings. This tradition is still practiced to some extent today. Why did they choose Lord's Prayer? I believe the answer is obvious—because the program uses God's Word as a template. Surprised? Don't be. When you read both *The Bible* and *The Big Book* of A.A., you will soon discover *The Big Book* and its teachings were directly derived from *The Bible*. Add to those Biblical teachings the common experiences of the alcoholic members themselves, and you have the most successful program ever to combat the plague of alcoholism.

This program's success is unquestioned, and is based on living in the Spirit, even if the alcoholic does not realize that fact in the beginning. This program is based on specific Biblical principles. Jesus did not argue with the alcoholic at this point. He provided a clear path to sobriety. With this program's teachings, the Holy Spirit can lead the alcoholic to spiritual truths, and in time, Jesus Christ. Jesus does not split hairs here regarding who should receive credit for these truths. He simply created the answer to one of the most complex puzzles, and has done what He promised to do in Matthew 9:12-13: *"But when Jesus heard this, He said, 'It is not those who are healthy who need a physician, but those who are sick. (13) But go and learn what this means:* "I DESIRE COMPASSION, AND NOT SACRIFICE," *for I did not come to call the righteous, but sinners.'"* The evidence that Jesus Christ loves alcoholics is the A.A. program. Even if alcoholics refuse to recognize God's hand in all this, He still loves them, and the Holy Spirit will still try to drive the alcoholic to Him.

Those who have never been to an A.A. meeting may speculate if we discuss Jesus Christ at an A.A. meeting. No, many alcoholics would not attend the meetings at all if for even a moment they thought the program was just another religious form. I am confident the Holy Spirit will work to present Jesus Christ to the members of A. A. in His time, and usually through another Christian member. It is important that our beliefs, just as with the program of A.A., should be one of attraction, not promotion. I do not find it surprising the majority of A.A. meetings are held in Christian churches. That connection is natural. The church provides a place to meet where the Spirit of God is always active. The church and A.A. complement each other well and never need to compete with each other. I have heard many A.A. members say they do not go to church because it is just a man-made fabrication. That simply is not true. The church was Jesus Christ's idea, not the idea of men. Look what Jesus said in Matthew 16:18: "I also say to you that you are Peter, and upon this rock I will build My church; and the gates of Hades will not overpower it." I just thought you should know that.

The most important point I can make in this book is to let you know if you are counting on your sobriety as your entrance to Heaven, rather than Jesus Christ, think again. Even if you manage to stay sober, (and it is with His help, whether you know it or not), but you ignore Jesus Christ in your life, you will still die in your sins, eternally separated from God. Jesus Christ promises in John 8:24, *"Therefore I said to you that you will die in your sins; for unless you believe that I am He, you will die in your sins."*

Even if you gain sobriety, and life seems pretty good, you still have an extremely valuable decision to make. Christ asked in Matthew 16:26, *"For what will it profit a man if he gains the whole world and forfeits his soul? Or what will a man give in exchange for his soul?"* I would rather die drinking and be in Christ, then to die sober without Him. I am not being sarcastic, but am trying to drive home a point here. If you die without accepting Jesus Christ's forgiveness for your sin, you have just sealed your eternal destiny. Think about that. Forever is a long time. There is nothing—and I mean nothing—that is more important to a human being, than this decision. Now is the time to deal with this issue. According to II Corinthians 6:2, *"for He says,* 'AT THE ACCEPTABLE TIME I LISTENED TO YOU, AND ON THE DAY OF SALVATION I HELPED YOU.' *Behold, now is* 'THE ACCEPTABLE TIME,' *behold, now is* 'THE DAY OF SALVATION.'" There will be no second chance. No reincarnation. *The Bible* states after death, comes judgment in Hebrews 9:27, *"And inasmuch as it is appointed for men to die once and after this comes judgment."* Judgment Day will come whether you choose Christ or not. Where will you be?

Remember, A.A. even teaches that it is a spiritual oriented program, and so it is. Most of the twelve steps are spiritually based. In fact, the whole A.A. program is spiritual in nature. I challenge you to read *The Bible* then listen to what is said and taught in A.A. It won't take any alcoholic too long to see the connection between the A.A. program and the Biblical God. All one has to do is be aware of God's leading, and the Spirit of God will take care of the rest. I just ask that you keep an open mind. I know you will be glad you did.

Chapter 4

Satan and the World

We talked about the role of the Holy Spirit in a Christian's life, and the importance of the Spirit's control for the alcoholic. In contrast, it is important to understand the part Satan plays in the life of the alcoholic. You may question if Satan has a genuine role or has an active force in the life of the alcoholic. He certainly does. Alcoholics Anonymous further declares in their manual, the *Big Book*, they are a spiritual program, and Satan is a big part of the spiritual realm. Whether alcoholics know it or not, Satan is the one who sets us up and keeps us drunk. We give him all the cooperation he will ever need. We may not want to talk about Satan or deal with him, but that does not make him any less real. In fact, not believing in his existence or his active role in this world plays right into his hands. The reason most alcoholics cannot obtain sobriety, is that they do not understand that their real battle is a spiritual battle. The Alcoholics

Anonymous program understands this concept all too well, and so does the church. The alcoholic must battle the physical, emotional, and mental aspects of alcoholism, but the battle to get well is definitely spiritual. Satan knows who you are, and he is here, as we can read in Job 1:7, *"The LORD said to Satan, 'From where do you come?' Then Satan answered the LORD and said, 'From roaming about on the earth and walking around on it.'"* The Devil is not only here in this world; according to Ephesians 2:2, he is also a formidable force; *"In which you formerly walked according to the course of this world, according to the prince of the power of the air, of the spirit that is now working in the sons of disobedience."*

Knowing that Satan exists in this world and is actively working against Christ in people's lives is not enough. You need to know if he can be stopped, or if there is any way or any one that can discourage him from continually ruining our lives. There is One Who can protect us against Satan, and that is Jesus Christ. Jesus gives us the Holy Spirit to engage Satan in battle—and it will be a battle. Remember I previously mentioned Satan is no match for the Holy Spirit. When Jesus was here on this earth, He knocked Satan around every at chance He got. Satan tried to tempt Jesus in the desert, but to no avail. Let's look at that passage from Matthew 4:1-11:

(1) Then Jesus was led up by the Spirit into the wilderness to be tempted by the devil. (2) And after He had fasted forty days and forty nights, He then became hungry. (3) And the tempter came and said to Him, "If You are the Son of God, command that these stones become bread." (4) But He answered and said, "It is written, 'MAN SHALL NOT LIVE ON BREAD ALONE, BUT ON EVERY WORD THAT PROCEEDS OUT OF THE MOUTH OF GOD.'" *(5) Then the devil took Him into the holy city and had Him stand on the pinnacle of the temple, (6) and said to Him, "If You are the Son of God, throw Yourself down; for it is written,* 'HE WILL COMMAND HIS ANGELS CONCERNING YOU'; *and* 'ON *their* HANDS THEY WILL BEAR YOU UP, SO THAT YOU WILL NOT STRIKE YOUR FOOT AGAINST A STONE.'" *(7) Jesus said to him, "On the other hand, it is written,* 'YOU SHALL NOT PUT THE LORD YOUR GOD TO THE TEST.'" *(8) Again, the devil took Him to a very high mountain and showed Him all the kingdoms of the world and their glory; (9) and he said to Him, "All these things I will give You, if You fall down and worship me." (10)*

> *Then Jesus said to him, "Go, Satan! For it is written, 'YOU SHALL WORSHIP THE LORD YOUR GOD, AND SERVE HIM ONLY.'" (11) Then the devil left Him; and behold, angels came and began to minister to Him.*

Satan and the other demons do not look forward to any encounters with Jesus or the Holy Spirit. You can see that point corroborated in this passage from Matthew 8:28-34:

> *(28) When He came to the other side into the country of the Gadarenes, two men who were demon-possessed met Him as they were coming out of the tombs. They were so extremely violent that no one could pass by that way. (29) And they cried out, saying, "What business do we have with each other, Son of God? Have You come here to torment us before the time?" (30) Now there was a herd of many swine feeding at a distance from them. (31) The demons began to entreat Him, saying, "If You are going to cast us out, send us into the herd of swine." (32) And He said to them, "Go!" And they came out and went into the swine, and the whole herd rushed down the steep bank into the sea and perished in the waters. (33) The herdsmen ran away, and went to the city and reported everything, including what had*

> *happened to the demoniacs. (34) And behold, the whole city came out to meet Jesus; and when they saw Him, they implored Him to leave their region.*

Satan is a big part of the alcoholic's battle. According to I Peter 5:8, we are to *"Be of sober spirit, be on the alert; your adversary, the devil, prowls around like a roaring lion, seeking someone to devour."* If a person is walking in the Spirit, they do not need to fear Satan. You should definitely be aware of the Devil, but you do not need to fear him. If we continuously rely on the strength of the Holy Spirit, even though we know it will be a battle at times, we can overcome Satan as well as our addiction. The alcoholic must first want sobriety, and as discussed previously, they must learn to live in the Spirit. If you begin to live in the Spirit, over time Satan will start to back away from you—not because it is you, but because he just cannot compete with the Holy Spirit. You should also remember this point though; Satan and alcoholism are the perfect match. The alcoholic's struggle is indeed Satan's arena. Unless the alcoholic is actively living in the Spirit, Satan will do whatever he has to do to get the alcoholic drunk and keep them there. The alcoholic must be in Christ's family, and living in the Spirit. As long as you stay connected to the church, your A.A. meetings, *The Bible*, and *The Big Book* of A.A., and genuinely pray for God's help, you will prevail. If there are some exceptions to rule, I have never seen one.

Alcoholism is a spiritual disease. Alcoholics Anonymous repeatedly confirms that idea. So does it not make sense to fight that disease with all the spiritual weapons we have available? I cannot defeat Satan or find sobriety on my own, but I do know Jesus Christ and the Holy Spirit can defeat him; and now, so do you.

Chapter 5

Evil—What It Is and Does

The next few chapters will deal with some specific spiritual matters from *The Bible*. Satan does not want the alcoholic to know anything about evil, salvation, or anything else that is spiritually related. Satan does not want you to know what *The Bible* says about this life and what surely will come after it. *The Big Book* of A.A. deals with living here on this earth, now, in the present; however you need to know what comes after an alcoholic dies and leaves this world. The Alcoholics Anonymous meetings do not address the reality of the afterlife, but *The Bible* does. Understanding that idea is very important. In the next few chapters, you will discover why it is important to understand what happens after a person dies.

You may wonder why I want to talk about evil, or what the point is to talking about this topic. The point is the alcoholic is fighting a spiritual battle, and evil is a big part of that battle. If you do not know what evil is, and how it affects your life, how can you properly fight it? As the old saying goes, "Know your enemy."

As alcoholism progresses in a person's life, evil will seem normal and that is why I am going to talk about it. Evil may seem too harsh a word, but ask yourself if it really is. Perhaps to the alcoholic, that word may sound too dramatic, but not to the people who have to deal and live with the alcoholic. Alcoholism, especially in its final stages, truly becomes evil in nature. The alcoholic must find a way to become honest about this fact. Additionally, the alcoholic must see alcoholism for the vicious disease it is, and not what they wish it was. I am not saying the alcoholic is evil, I am saying the behavior of the alcoholic becomes evil when they are drinking. You may use words other than evil to describe alcoholic behavior, such as sin, poor judgment, wrong choices, or my favorite—misguided.

The truth is that alcoholism kills too many people, leaves too many children with only one parent, puts too many people in jail, and causes more tears and heartbreak than any other disease on this planet. I would call that *evil*. Let's further define the concept of evil.

In my own definition, evil is sin that is allowed to prosper and grow until it takes on a dimension that rational people have trouble even comprehending. That was the situation in the days of Noah, as we read in Genesis 6:5, *"Then the LORD saw that the wickedness of man was great on the earth, and that every intent of the thoughts of his heart was only evil continually."*

Evil is selfish, self-serving, and does not care about honesty, feelings, or anything else for that matter. It will do whatever it takes to get what it wants. It is self-centeredness perfected. Above all, evil has no conscience, so right and wrong is never an issue. Evil is only concerned with getting what it wants, or what it thinks it needs. What I have just written accurately describes my state of mind or actions when I am drinking. I would do or say just about anything and run over anyone I have to, so I could keep on drinking. If I had to lie, I would lie. If I had to manipulate someone so that I could continue to drink, so be it. When I needed to drink, the gloves came off. Anything—and I mean *anything* went. At that point in my alcoholic state, I had lost the ability to stay in the Spirit. When a person is drunk, living in the Spirit is just not going to happen and cannot be done. You can confirm this in Romans 8:7-8, where we are told *"because the mind set on the flesh* (addiction) *is hostile toward God; for it does not subject itself to the law of God, for it is not even able to do so, (8) and those who are in the flesh* (active addiction) *cannot please God."* Believe me; I have personally tried to please God while I was in a state of active addiction, so I know that it cannot be done.

I do not want to preach to any one. That is certainly not my intent, but just like alcoholism, evil has consequences. So I am going to mention the subject of Hell, because if a person does not have Jesus Christ in their life, I think it would be a place a person would want to know about, since it will be their last stop. I know—people do not like to hear this type of thing, and to tell you the truth, I do not like writing about it; however, for many people, Hell will be a reality. I hope it will not be a reality for you, but it will be for majority of people. Look what Jesus said in Matthew 7:14: *"For the gate is small and the way is narrow that leads to life, and there are few who find it."*

What exactly is Hell then? Hell is literal place that separates the sinner from God, and anything decent or good. In 2 Thessalonians 1:9 we read that about those individuals who go to Hell, that *"These will pay the penalty of eternal destruction, away from the presence of the Lord and from the glory of His power."* There you will find no love, no trust, no caring, and above all, no truth. Welcome to the great Liefest! Hypocrisy and lawlessness abound there, and you will be in a constant state of sadness and fear. See what The Bible says in Matthew 25:30: *"Throw out the worthless slave into the outer darkness; in that place there will be weeping and gnashing of teeth."* Jesus Christ's parable in Luke 16:24 further tells us about the rich man's experience in Hell, stating the rich man *"...cried out and said, 'Father Abraham, have mercy on me, and send Lazarus so that he may dip the tip of his finger in water and cool off my tongue, for I am in agony in this flame.'"*

Hell is a real place with real people. You won't die there. You won't be that fortunate. Instead, you will live and breathe in constant torment. I am not trying to scare anyone. I just think people should be informed. On this earth there is much goodness to offset the evil, but in Hell, that will not be the case.

As I stated earlier in my introduction, I am writing this book from a Huber unit of the Rock County Jail. I am here because of drinking and driving. I deserve to be here. The only positive aspect I can find here is that I believe God allowed me to catch a glimpse of the situation in Hell. I am an alcoholic. I am a Viet Nam veteran, yet I have never seen or experienced anything like this place before. Almost everything I have described in this chapter exists in this jail. I have never, and I mean never, seen people talk to and treat one another the way they do in this place. Except for a precious few individuals, this place is evil. It is horrible. I cannot believe what I hear and see. No truth. No caring. No respect for authority. "Do what is best for you, and don't care about anyone else" and "squash people who cannot defend themselves" are the basic mind-sets here. This must simply be a glimpse of Hell. Very little that is good exists here to challenge the evil, and that is the reality of Hell. Evil does what evil says it is going to do. I am not saying the inmates themselves are evil, but the behavior here is just awful. I am glad this chapter is over.

Chapter 6

The Alcoholic and Salvation or Judgment

It is important to me that everyone who is reading this book understand what I am trying to convey in this chapter, but it is especially important the alcoholic understands this chapter well. If you believe in Jesus Christ and trust him, Heaven is your next and final stop. We are told clearly in *The Bible* in Romans 10:9, *"that if you confess with your mouth Jesus as Lord, and believe in your heart that God raised Him from the dead, you will be saved."* The reason I say "especially the alcoholic" is that if an alcoholic relapses, and engages in active drinking they may believe they have automatically been sentenced to Hell. If an alcoholic thinks that way, they may never even want to seek help. *What would be the point? I am going to Hell anyway*, they think. It is particularly difficult for an alcoholic to remember they are a child of God while the alcohol is destroying them. We are assured in John 1:12, *"But as many as received Him, to them He gave the right to become children of God, even to those who believe in His name."* Although this statement is a fact, it is not a license to drink. If you drink, you will suffer, and I mean *suffer*! Alcoholism is a progressive disease. It never levels off. It gets worse and as we discussed, God will not shield you from the consequences of your drinking. We can see that point in Galatians 6:7, which states: *"Do not be deceived, God is not mocked; for whatever a man sows, this he will also reap."* The alcoholic, or any person, for that matter, must remember there is a spiritual battle going on for their soul. The Spirit of God will not force Himself on you, or force you to do anything against your will. God gave us freedom of choice—the right to choose what we will do with the gift He offers. If we ignore the Holy Spirit, and do not want Him, He will leave us alone until He is asked back. You might wonder what happens after a person chooses to ignore the Holy Spirit. I believe their life will get worse. Look at this verse from Matthew 12:45, *"Then it goes and takes along with it seven other spirits more wicked than itself, and they go in and live there; and the last state of that man becomes worse than the first. That is the way it will also be with this evil generation."* The common denominator you will hear when alcoholics relapse is that their drinking that time was worse than it was before they stopped. Now you know why.

Salvation is a free gift. It is not based on what a person does or does not do. Salvation is based on One individual alone—Jesus Christ. Many people, even many Christians struggle with this concept. Christians struggle with understanding that once they have accepted that gift, they do not have to keep trying to earn it. It is free. That is the beginning and the end of the story. The issue is settled if you believe and trust Jesus like He told the woman in John 11:25-26, *"Jesus said to her, 'I am the resurrection and the life; he who believes in Me will live even if he dies, (26) and everyone who lives and believes in Me will never die. Do you believe this?'"* This may sound too good to be true, but it is true. Drinking cannot nullify your salvation, just as sobriety cannot obtain it. We are assured in Ephesians 2:8-9, *"For by grace you have been saved through faith; and that not of yourselves, it is the gift of God; (9) not as a result of works, so that no one may boast."*

Sobriety is the best way to live and exist on this earth. I could give an alcoholic a hundred good reasons to stay sober, and not one good reason to drink. I destroyed my life by drinking. Don't do the same. If I had listened to what I am writing now, alcohol would not have had the chance to do to me what it has done. I hope someone, somewhere learns from this.

Next, I will discuss the subject of Judgment Day because people need to know about this concept as well. Once you have read what I have to say, and what God's Word has to say, you can at least make an informed decision regarding how you are going to deal with the subject. It has always amazed me how people can just ignore all these truths! How can anyone put their eternal destiny at risk? Eternity is forever. That is a long time. Are the few years we spend on this earth that important? How can any thinking person not see the trade-off? Judgment Day will come, and when it does, it is going to be a horrible, horrible day. Jesus talked about "the weeping and gnashing of teeth" on that day. That means sheer fear, and what makes it even worse, is there is no second chance. You will not be able to talk your way out of that event, or play dumb, saying you "did not know any better," since God says in Romans 1:19-20 that you did know better, *"because that which is known about God is evident within them; for God made it evident to them. (20) For since the creation of the world His invisible attributes, His eternal power and divine nature, have been clearly seen, being understood through what has been made, so that they are without excuse."* Again, I am not preaching. I am trying to help you. Jesus tolerated a lot of bad behavior, but He did not tolerate being ignored. I have heard it often said that when a person goes to Heaven they will see several people they would not expect to see, and will not see several people they thought they would. Jesus told a parable to illustrate this point in Luke 16:19-31:

> *(19) Now there was a rich man, and he habitually dressed in purple and fine linen, joyously living in splendor every day. (20) And a poor man named Lazarus was laid at his gate, covered with sores, and longing to be fed with the crumbs which were falling from the rich man's table; besides, even the dogs were coming and licking his sores. (22) Now the poor man died and was carried away by the angels to Abraham's bosom; and the rich man also died and was buried. (23) In Hades he lifted up his eyes, being in torment, and saw Abraham far away and Lazarus in his bosom. (24) And he cried out and said, 'Father Abraham, have mercy on me, and send Lazarus so that he may dip the tip of his finger in water and cool off my tongue, for I am in agony in this flame.' (25) But Abraham said, 'Child, remember that during your life you received your good things, and likewise Lazarus bad things; but now he is being comforted here, and you are in agony. (26) 'And besides all this, between us and you there is a great chasm fixed, so that those who wish to come over from here to you*

will not be able, and that none may cross over from there to us.' (27) And he said, 'Then I beg you, father, that you send him to my father's house-- (28) for I have five brothers--in order that he may warn them, so that they will not also come to this place of torment.' (29) But Abraham said, 'They have Moses and the Prophets; let them hear them.' (30) But he said, 'No, father Abraham, but if someone goes to them from the dead, they will repent!' (31) But he said to him, 'If they do not listen to Moses and the Prophets, they will not be persuaded even if someone rises from the dead.'

Lazarus may have been a poor man, but he was a believer. The rich man seemed to be a decent man, and even expressed concerned about his family's destiny after his death, but he was not a believer before he died. Perhaps the rich man just put that decision off, choosing not to deal with Jesus or judgment. He did not have a good ending, did he? The rich man ignored God, and a person simply cannot do that. If you want Jesus Christ in your life, He will be there. If you just want to control your own life in another direction, you can choose that path as well. Like my dad used to say, "You can do or be anything you want, as long as you're willing to deal with the consequences." If you choose not to deal with Jesus Christ and judgment, you had better make your remaining years on this earth count—really count. Jesus spent more time teaching about salvation and judgment than He did on just about anything else. I believe He had a very good reason for that—so that you can make the right choice for your life.

There are two types of judgments. The first judgment is for the believer, and it is the Judgment Seat of Christ that we read about in 2 Corinthians 5:16, *"For we must all appear before the judgment seat of Christ, so that each one may be recompensed for his deeds in the body, according to what he has done, whether good or bad."* The good or bad deeds that Jesus is referring to in this verse are not referring to a person's sins, because those have been forgiven and forgotten. What Christ is talking about in this passage is how we as Christians used our lives. We will be assessed on whether we told others about Christ, or if we helped other people, or even if we cared enough about other people. We are told about that day in Matthew 25:40, and it says *"The King will answer and say to them, 'Truly I say to you, to the extent that you did it to one of these brothers of Mine, even the least of them, you did it to Me.'"* Recovering alcoholics are often a fine example of someone who is willing to help another person. They make themselves readily available to the alcoholic who is still suffering whenever they are needed. Whether they are aware of it or not, they are doing exactly what Jesus would have them do. The

Holy Spirit can use those individuals to reach the alcoholic and help alcoholics as they begin their journey toward recovery.

The second judgment is the Great White Throne Judgment. That is the judgment for the unbelievers, as we see in Revelation 20:11-15:

> *(11) Then I saw a great white throne and Him who sat upon it, from whose presence earth and heaven fled away, and no place was found for them. (12) And I saw the dead, the great and the small, standing before the throne, and books were opened; and another book was opened, which is the book of life; and the dead were judged from the things which were written in the books, according to their deeds. (13) And the sea gave up the dead which were in it, and death and Hades gave up the dead which were in them; and they were judged, every one of them according to their deeds. (14) Then death and Hades were thrown into the lake of fire. This is the second death, the lake of fire. (15) And if anyone's name was not found written in the book of life, he was thrown into the lake of fire.*

Those that have already accepted Jesus Christ in their lives do not enter this judgment, just the unbelievers. Those individuals will have to answer for every one of their sins. This will not be a happy time. It will be a heartbreaking and awful event. For so many people, it will never be any worse. I urge you to deal with Jesus Christ now and stay out of that courtroom.

In closing, I want to emphasize that God takes no delight in the eternal damnation of anyone. This is certainly not his desire, as He tells us in Ezekiel 18:32, *"For I have no pleasure in the death of anyone who dies," declares the Lord GOD. "Therefore, repent and live."* God wants everyone to be part of His family, and sent His Son, Jesus, to die for everyone, but the problem is not everyone wants Him in their lives. God is loving; however, He cannot allow an unbeliever, who has rejected His Son's sacrifice, into Heaven. God has two traits that one should never forget, according to Romans 11:22, *"Behold then the kindness and severity of God; to those who fell, severity, but to you, God's kindness, if you continue in His kindness; otherwise you also will be cut off."* It is up to you. It is just that simple.

Chapter 7

How I See Jesus

For you to better understand why I trust so much in Jesus Christ, I want you to see Him as I do. The only way you can understand who Jesus Christ is, is to see what is written about Him in His Book, *The Bible*. He is God—John 10:30: *"I and the Father are one."* He is the Creator—John 1:3: *"All things came into being through Him, and apart from Him nothing came into being that has come into being."* He is a teacher—Matthew 10:24: *"A disciple is not above his teacher, nor a slave above his master."* He is humanity's one, true hope for eternal destiny—Matthew 18:11: *"For the Son of Man has come to save that which was lost."* He is also a man, and at critical times showed that fact—Luke 22:44: *"And being in agony He was praying very fervently; and His sweat became like drops of blood, falling down upon the ground."* During the three years of His public ministry, He was homeless—Matthew 8:20:

"Jesus said to him, "The foxes have holes and the birds of the air have nests, but the Son of Man has nowhere to lay His head." He displayed signs and miracles of which only God could be attributed. He walked on the water—Mark 6:49: *"But when they saw Him walking on the sea, they supposed that it was a ghost, and cried out."* He could control the weather—Luke 8:24: *"They came to Jesus and woke Him up, saying, 'Master, Master, we are perishing!' And He got up and rebuked the wind and the surging waves, and they stopped, and it became calm."* He restored sight to the blind—Luke 18:42-43: *"And Jesus said to him, 'Receive your sight; your faith has made you well.' (43) Immediately he regained his sight and began following Him, glorifying God; and when all the people saw it, they gave praise to God."* He could command the spirits—Matthew 9:33: *"After the demon was cast out, the mute man spoke; and the crowds were amazed, and were saying, 'Nothing like this has ever been seen in Israel.'"* He touched the lives of more people than we could ever imagine—John 21:25: *"And there were also many other things which Jesus did, which if they were written in detail, I suppose that even the world itself could not contain the books that would be written."* He raised people from the dead—John 11:43-44: *"When He had said these things, He cried out with a loud voice, 'Lazarus, come forth.' (44) The man who had died came forth, bound hand and foot with wrappings,*

and his face was wrapped around with a cloth. Jesus said to them, 'Unbind him, and let him go.'" Most importantly, He personally rose from the dead, and after all of that, many people still would not believe—John 20:25: *"So the other disciples were saying to him, 'We have seen the Lord!' But he said to them, 'Unless I see in His hands the imprint of the nails, and put my finger into the place of the nails, and put my hand into His side, I will not believe.'"* So is Jesus Christ, God? I believe He is without any doubt. There is simply too much evidence and too many witnesses. It would hold up in any court today with a fair hearing.

Jesus was also a mortal man, and without a speck of doubt, the greatest man that had or ever would set foot on this earth. He is just amazing. He had to have a sense of humor, as evidenced by some of the nicknames He gave his disciples. He seemed to have a lot of fun with James and John. He nicknamed them the "Sons of Thunder" (Mark 3:17), since they were the "shoot now, ask questions later" type of men. We can see a great example of those two men's personality trait in Luke 9:54-56 when they ask, *"When His disciples James and John saw this, they said, 'Lord, do You want us to command fire to come down from heaven and consume them?' (55) But He turned and rebuked them, and said, 'You do not know what kind of spirit you are of.' (56) for the Son of Man did not come to destroy men's lives, but to save them.' And they went on to another village."*

Jesus even demonstrated irritation at times, especially with his disciples. Look at this passage in Mark 8:17-18: *"And Jesus, aware of this, said to them, "Why do you discuss the fact that you have no bread? Do you not yet see or understand? Do you have a hardened heart? (18)* 'HAVING EYES, DO YOU NOT SEE? AND HAVING EARS, DO YOU NOT HEAR? *And do you not remember.'"* He became particularly irritated when people were using the temple for a buy-and-sell shop, as we can read in Matthew 21:12-13: *"And Jesus entered the temple and drove out all those who were buying and selling in the temple, and overturned the tables of the money changers and the seats of those who were selling doves. (13) And He said to them, 'It is written,* "MY HOUSE SHALL BE CALLED A HOUSE OF PRAYER"; *but you are making it a* ROBBERS' DEN.'"

It seems he was beyond irritated with the Jewish Scribes and Pharisees, who were the religious hierarchy, and he let them know quite clearly how he viewed their actions toward people. Among other names, he called those men in Matthew 23:13-36, hypocrites, sons of Hell, blind guides, fools, blind men, serpents, and a brood of vipers! Nowhere else in the Gospels did a person or group of people stir the wrath of Jesus the way the Scribes and Pharisees did. It seems he was incensed by them. If it was any other mortal man except for Jesus saying those things, we would probably have called it a tirade. Jesus just did not tolerate self-righteous, arrogant people. Those people saw no need for Him and His ministry. He loved and worked with the people who knew they had problems, who knew their life was not right, wanted and believed in Him. As He always said, they were the ones who needed Him the most.

Jesus also felt pain. He knew what it was like not to want to suffer and die. In Matthew 26:38 we read, *"Then He said to them, 'My soul is deeply grieved, to the point of death; remain here and keep watch with Me.'"* Most alcoholics can tell you that of all the trials and feelings they must endure and deal with, loneliness is by far the most difficult emotion to have to face. As Jesus could attest to even at his death, he declared his feelings of abandonment by God the Father as we read in Mark 15:34, *"At the ninth hour Jesus cried out with a loud voice,* 'ELOI, ELOI, LAMA SABACHTHANI?'" *which is translated,* 'MY GOD, MY GOD, WHY HAVE YOU FORSAKEN ME?'" Jesus knew the feeling of loneliness all too well, a feeling to which the alcoholic can often relate. We should take comfort in the fact that Jesus does know how we feel. He has been there.

Jesus spent most His time in the temple and synagogues teaching and praying. He also spent time going from town to town teaching. In fact, according to *The Bible*, Jesus went to about every town and village to where one could walk. He also spent time in the rural areas such as the place where He performed his miracle of feeding over five thousand people.

The people Jesus spent His time with were most often His disciples, the people in the temples, and particularly the everyday people, and not just the cream-of-the-crop individuals either. Jesus spent a great amount of time with people just like us—drunks. In fact, He was even accused of being a drunk in Matthew 11:19, *"The Son of Man came eating and drinking, and they say, 'Behold, a gluttonous man and a drunkard, a friend of tax collectors and sinners!' Yet wisdom is vindicated by her deeds."* Did Jesus drink? Jesus says He did. I believe He did drink alcohol in fact. Some people believe the wine He drank, and the wine that He made at the wedding feast was nonalcoholic; however, *The Bible* does not say the wine was nonalcoholic. I believe He drank alcohol in moderation, just like 90% of the people who drink it today do. I believe He knew what it was like. He did not get drunk, and certainly was not an alcoholic, but I believe He could relate to the drinking. I think Jesus spent all this time with the harlots, drunks, and the people who could not control their behavior and addictions, because Jesus said they were the ones who needed Him the most—then and now. I am sure Jesus was well aware of how addiction could destroy a person. I am also sure He understood the utter loneliness of that destructive behavior, and that is why He spent as much time as He did with the drunks, harlots and other people with addictions and sin problems. He was aware most people, even one's own family, would leave the alcoholic to fend for themselves; not because those people did not love the alcoholic, but they did not want to be destroyed by the alcoholic's behavior. Even if friends and family did not fear for themselves, it is just too difficult to watch a person go through that situation. Jesus addressed those people with addictions and destructive behavior directly. He met people on their own turf. I think if Jesus were with us on this earth today, I am sure some of His time would be spent in the tavern—not getting drunk, but by His mere presence, demonstrating his concern for the alcoholic and nonalcoholic alike. His death on the cross was for people just like you and me as I demonstrated with the cover of this book.

Jesus had a charisma that attracted large crowds, as we can see in Matthew 15:30, *"And large crowds came to Him..."* And it was not His rugged good looks that attracted people. Isaiah 53:2 states, *"...He has no stately form of majesty that we should look upon Him, nor appearance that we should be attracted to Him."* Jesus had a message of hope, of healing and concern. Any one with an open heart and mind found security in Him, yet there were still people who did not like Him. Those people both feared and envied Him. Many religious leaders thought they knew more than Jesus did, and according to Scriptures, He did not seem to appreciate that attitude either. Let's look at a passage from John 9:40-41, "Those of the Pharisees who were with Him heard these things and said to Him, *'We are not blind too, are we?' (41) Jesus said to them, 'If you were blind, you would have no sin; but since you say, 'We see,' your sin remains.*"

No matter how much evidence Jesus provided, no matter how many miracles He performed, many people just did not want to accept Him. That fact remains every bit as true still today. It is a terrible shame, but that is the way life is. The truth is some people just get addicted to themselves and this world. As an alcoholic, I should be able to understand that idea, but I fear for people's lives because the stakes are so high.

In closing this chapter, as a mortal man, Jesus knew the type of death He was going to die. He knew it would be humiliating, brutal, and sadistic. They beat Him half to death before they even crucified Him. Those people were barbaric in their treatment of this man! Those people tortured Him in every possible way that they could, and He just endured it. One should not be surprised while praying in the Garden of Gethsemane faced with the thought of the torture and death he would soon encounter,

His sweat came out as drops of blood. We can be assured that if His Father was willing to endorse the idea of Jesus escaping that death on the cross, Jesus would have walked away. Jesus was willing to do what He was sent to this earth to accomplish, but still asked His Father in Matthew 26:39 if there was any other possible solution: *"And He went a little beyond them, and fell on His face and prayed, saying, 'My Father, if it is possible, let this cup pass from Me; yet not as I will, but as You will.'"*

We should all remember Jesus had a choice whether to sacrifice His life for the world. He just chose not to exercise that choice—and that is very good news for all mankind. He knew that if He asked His Father to remove Him from the cross, God would have sent legions of angels to rescue Him. He states that clearly in Matthew 26:53-54, when He answered the jeering crowd, *"'Or do you think that I cannot appeal to My Father, and He will at once put at My disposal more than twelve legions of angels? (54) How then will the Scriptures be fulfilled, which say that it must happen this way?'"* How can anyone ignore the Person Who would sacrifice their life for them? To me, Jesus is first and foremost, God. He is my Savior, my hope, and probably more than anything, He is my best friend, as He declares in John 15:13, *"No longer do I call you slaves, for the slave does not know what his master is doing; but I have called you friends, for all things that I have heard from My Father I have made known to you."*

There have been many times in my life which I have been a very poor Christian. In fact, they have been way too many times. Often, I was not true to my calling. I did not act on what I knew to be true. I am certain if it were not for Jesus' sacrifice, my condemnation would be sure. I was given several good people in my life, and several good things, yet I did little to retain them. I was too selfish, too stupid, and I wanted to do my own thing—drink, and that has destroyed me. I will say on my own behalf though, I never denied Jesus Christ as my Savior. We are told in Matthew 10:33, *"But whoever denies Me before men, I will also deny him before My Father who is in heaven."* I have also never been ashamed of Jesus, because Mark 8:38 states, *"For whoever is ashamed of Me and My words in this adulterous and sinful generation, the Son of Man will also be ashamed of him when He comes in the glory of His Father with the holy angels."* I have never lost my respect or my view of Jesus. Yes, Jesus was and is amazing, and most certainly one of a kind. I cannot wait to meet him.

Chapter 8

The Brevity of Life

I have talked about Heaven and Hell after your life on this earth ends, but perhaps you still have questions about this life. How do we view this life, as opposed to how God looks at it? Do we see it the same way? I think not. A good explanation of how God sees this life can be found in Isaiah 55:8, "*'For My thoughts are not your thoughts, nor are your ways My ways,' declares the LORD.*" We hold a time and space view of life by which God is not bound. *The Bible* reveals in 2 Peter 3:8, "*But do not let this one fact escape your notice, beloved, that with the Lord one day is like a thousand years, and a thousand years like one day.*" Our flesh and our instincts may tell us that this present life is all we have, or that our life on earth is the most important part of one's total existence. So many people fear death so much because they believe that view. Jesus taught that our life here is important, but not nearly as important as our eternal existence.

He told His disciples in Matthew 10:28, *"Do not fear those who kill the body, but are unable to kill the soul, but rather fear him who is able to destroy both soul and body in Hell."*

Jesus tried to teach people to set their priorities in the correct order. We have a difficult time accepting this teaching about proper priorities. God takes the long view of life, and we almost always take the short view, and that is why the idea of death has the hold on us that it does. If we somehow can start to look at our life here as a small part of our total existence, we would be on the road to becoming significantly more secure.

Before you can begin to comprehend God's view about our time on earth, perhaps you need see how brief our stay is. That time is brief in contrast to eternity. According to Psalm 39:5 the writer declared, *"Behold, You have made my days as handbreadths, and my lifetime as nothing in Your sight; surely every man at his best is a mere breath. Selah."* We may feel or think earth is our home, but in reality, it is not. For a Christian, Heaven is home. The Apostle Paul rejoiced in 2 Corinthians 5:8 by writing, *"We are of good courage, I say, and prefer rather to be absent from the body and to be at home with the Lord."* Paul had no doubt about where his true home was. The apostle even shared if it were not for the special commission Jesus had given him, he was not shy in telling the church where he would have preferred to be. Philippians 1:21-23, *"For to me, to live is Christ and to die is gain. (22) But if I am to live on in the flesh, this will mean fruitful labor for me; and I do not know which to choose. (23) But I am hard-pressed from both directions, having the desire to depart and be with Christ, for that is very much better."* Paul never referred to this earth as home. He considered Heaven his home. That is the good news we can give to someone when a person dies who is a Christian. They are home. This news is not a hope or a wish, but a reality. If they were a Christian that loved one is with God, and they are far better off than we who are still alive on this earth. I always told my children if I were to die, they may grieve because they would miss me, and it would be difficult, but do not feel sorry for me. I will be better off than they are. I told them further that they should be sad for themselves, but not for me.

Some people might wonder what they should say when an unbeliever dies. Honestly, I say nothing. It bothers me to know that person died an unbeliever. I hate visitations or funerals when I believe or suspect the person who died was an unbeliever. All you can do is pray that they were a believer, and you did not know it. If you cared for them, you pray, you hope.

Sometimes when I read *The Bible* and even *The Big Book* of A.A., I come away with the impression that everyone who believes and lives in the Spirit will eventually ride off into the sunset. Life will be Camelot. Sure, there will be some struggles, but overall, I thought life would be good. Have you ever watched a Jerry Lewis telethon, or a Feed the Children commercial? Maybe you watched the news or read a newspaper? Did you ever see otherwise healthy people confined to a bed or a wheelchair for the rest of their lives? There is no sunset or Camelot for them. You may question why the world is this way, or what those people did to deserve that life. You may question the fairness of so many of the situations in this world, such as children who develop diseases, or babies born starving. All that sorrow can be enough to make a person sick, but no matter how we may all feel now, we must hold on to the fact much better things are just around the corner for those individuals and for all those who believe.

An entire book of *The Bible*, the book of Job is dedicated to this subject of suffering, and the unfairness of life. Job suffered like few people will ever have to, and through no fault of his own. Even though his story ended well, at the time of all his suffering, Job could not figure all the big questions out or why life would treat anyone like that. His wife got so upset with the whole situation she told Job to curse God. Read for yourself in Job 2:9: *"Then his wife said to him, 'Do you still hold fast to your integrity? Curse God and die!'"* Job did not curse God, but he had many questions for God regarding his suffering, and the inequity of life. God did not answer the question here of why life could be so cruel for some people and not fair for others. It appears God never gave Job the answer he wanted. God almost defies us to even question Him on this according to Isaiah 45:9, "*Woe to the one who quarrels with his Maker— an earthenware vessel among the vessels of earth! Will the clay say to the potter, 'What are you doing?' Or the thing you are making say, 'He has no hands'?*" Why do you think that God chose not to answer Job? I believe God has already given us the answer, but it is often an answer we simply refuse to accept.

Now you are probably curious what that answer may be. Life here on earth is not always fair. God's Word tells us in Matthew 5:45, "*so that you may be sons of your Father who is in heaven; for He causes His sun to rise on the evil and the good, and sends rain on the righteous and the unrighteous.*" Some people will have to endure more struggles, more injustice, more heartbreak, more pain, and more loss than others, including untimely deaths, disease, accidents, broken relationships and the list goes on. Life can be cruel. It can feel like it rips a person's heart out, but remember this, the more you have to endure, the more life is unfair to you, the more you have to suffer, the more tears you have to shed, and you continue to hold on to your faith, the greater your reward will be in

Heaven. We can read this in Isaiah 61:1-2, *"The Spirit of the Lord GOD is upon me, Because the LORD has anointed me to bring good news to the afflicted; He has sent me to bind up the brokenhearted, to proclaim liberty to captives and freedom to prisoners; (2) to proclaim the favorable year of the LORD and the day of vengeance of our God; to comfort all who mourn."* Many people who feel they are at the bottom of life now, will be at the top later according to Matthew 19:30, *"But many who are first will be last; and the last, first."*

Earlier I discussed the story of the rich man and Lazarus. That example from Jesus should help us all to remember that vindications are on their way for the believer. It should also remind everyone that even if one's life does go smoothly, it is not always an indication you have found favor with God. The rich man discovered that truth, but it was too late. No one should ever envy an unbeliever. *The Bible* tells us that many of the people who are so hurt and sad now, will be some of the happiest people in the kingdom of Heaven. We can rejoice in the words from Psalm 126:5-6, *"Those who sow in tears shall reap with joyful shouting. (6) He who goes to and fro weeping, carrying his bag of seed, shall indeed come again with a shout of joy, bringing his sheaves with him."*

You may ask how all this helps us at this point in your life. I think knowing the truth will help to some degree, but to many it may not help as much. Some people have a much higher mountain to climb and many more trials to overcome, but God promises those individuals will have their day. At that particular time, many of us will wish we were them.

I would like to address the topic of taking of one's own life—suicide? According to the 2003 statistics from the World Health Organization, over 35,000 people in United States alone die every year from suicide. There are many people, even many Christians that believe suicide is a mortal or unforgivable sin. Yes, suicide is a sin. It is murder by any definition, but it is a far from being an unforgivable sin. I would like to question where those people might base that belief. That belief cannot be founded on *The Bible*. Jesus does not talk about suicide being an unforgivable sin. Paul and Peter do not talk about it being unforgivable. No one does. You can try to take the Scripture out of context and try to apply them to fit that belief, or some people use the one particular Scripture reference out of context to support the idea that suicide is a mortal or unforgivable sin. That verse was written by Paul, and he stated in 1 Corinthians 3:16-17, "*Do you not know that you are a temple of God and that the Spirit of God dwells in you? (17) If any man destroys the temple of God, God will destroy him, for the temple of God is holy, and that is what you are.*" If one reads all of Chapter 3, you find out He is referring to the church as a whole, and not as individuals. 1

Corinthians 3:9, *"For we are God's fellow workers; you are God's field, God's building."* The temple Paul talks about here is the church as a whole, with Jesus Christ being the foundation. 1 Corinthians 3:11, *"For no one can lay any foundation other than the one already laid, which is Jesus Christ."* Paul was warning people not to try to destroy the church, which many people at that time were trying to do. He was not talking to individuals here concerning their own flesh and blood. In fact, Paul stated the only sin against one's own body is immorality, I Corinthians 6:18, *"Flee from sexual immorality. All other sins a man commits are outside his body, but he who sins sexually sins against his own body."* There is no evidence here, or anywhere else in *The Bible,* to support the claim suicide is an unforgivable sin. If one wants to make a case for sinning against their own body being an unforgivable sin, they would have to look at issues such as smoking, drinking, or even being a stunt pilot by putting their body at risk, obesity, not exercising, and the list could go on.

There are a few cases of culturally-related suicides in *The Bible* including Saul and his armor bearer in 1 Samuel 31:3-5, Ahithophel in 2 Samuel 17:23, as well as the guilt-ridden disciple Judas Iscariot in Matthew 27:5, among a few others. *The Bible* never stated, implied or referred to those individuals' eternal destiny because of their suicide. I firmly believe that if God wanted us to know suicide was an unforgivable sin, His Word would be the most likely place for Him to record that idea.

That brings us to the question of why *The Bible* seems strangely quiet on the topic of suicide. You may wonder why *The Bible* does not deal with the topic directly or why Jesus or Paul never taught on it. They did not need to reiterate the point that if the person who committed suicide was a believer, there was no question regarding their eternal destination. We can read in numerous places of The Bible such as John 6:47, where we are clearly told, "*Truly, truly, I say to you, he who believes has eternal life.*" There are no qualifications here. We can know for a fact any person who will enter the Kingdom of Heaven, will enter it by grace alone. Paul wrote in Ephesians 2:8-9, salvation was not based on what a person does or does not do, but is a gift, "*For by grace you have been saved through faith; and that not of yourselves, it is the gift of God; (9) not as a result of works, so that no one may boast.*"

If a believer, even one who has taken their own life, is sentenced to Hell, then we must question why Jesus had to die in the first place. Again the apostle Paul explains in Galatians 2:21 that "*I do not nullify the grace of God, for if righteousness comes through the Law, then Christ died needlessly.*" Christ died so all people could be saved by grace. At times, many of us seem to forget this fact. No one enters Heaven by what they do or do not do. *The Bible* makes that abundantly clear. Yes, there are Christians who do not fulfill their calling as believers, but that does not sentence them to Hell. That point is confirmed in 1 Corinthians 3:15 where it states: *"If any man's work is burned up, he will suffer loss; but he himself will be saved, yet so as through fire."* The most important thing to God is that we believe He is Who He says He is, and that we believe Jesus is God, and that He died for us so we may obtain salvation. See the verse from 1 Corinthians 15:3, *"For I delivered to you as of first importance what I also received, that Christ died for our sins according to the Scriptures."*

Anyone who may consider suicide an unforgivable sin should consider *The Bible* clearly states there is only one unforgivable sin in Matthew 12:31, where Jesus Christ says, *"'Therefore I say to you, any sin and blasphemy shall be forgiven people, but blasphemy against the Spirit shall not be forgiven.'"* The sin against the Spirit is apostasy—basically refusing to believe and deal with Jesus Christ. I have never personally met a Christian that believed murder is an unforgivable sin, so how can those same people believe suicide to be unforgivable? Does it make sense that one can take the life of an innocent person and be forgiven, but if a person takes their own life, they cannot be forgiven? That is not even logical. Anyone who believes suicide is an unforgivable sin should find Scripture to back that belief up, and they will spend their life looking for it, because it is simply not there. People should be careful when condemning other people to Hell without Scripture to back it up. Jesus taught in Matthew 7:1-2 not to judge other people, *"'Do not judge so that you will not be judged. (2) For in the way you judge, you will be judged; and by your standard of measure, it will be measured to you.'"* There is only one Judge for salvation, and we as humans are not that Judge. We would do well not to forget that fact which was reiterated in John 5:22, *"For not even the Father judges anyone, but He has given all judgment to the Son."*

If you are wondering why I spent so much time in this book on the topic of suicide, I will tell you there are two main reasons. First, in the later stages of alcoholism, the act of suicide can be a real possibility and it does occur. I believe people who commit suicide usually do so for one or more of the following reasons: the loss of something or someone; unbearable regret for past performance; fear of what they perceive the future to hold; and mental illness. Some people may say that suicide is a coward's way out of life; the person was simply weak; however, I don't agree that was the case at all. For one or more of the aforementioned reasons, that person lost all ability to cope with life as they knew it. No one wants to die, but sometimes the prospect of living could seem worse. Other people would tell you that they have wanted to commit suicide, but were too much of a coward to carry it out. I guess it just depends upon how one looks at the situation.

The second reason I felt this topic was important to understand is to relate to the person who has had a loved one, family member, friend or someone they cared about who has committed suicide, and they were told that person was destined to Hell. What a torture that must be to hear that garbage! How does one carry that burden? Again, I brought out Scriptural evidence to demonstrate *The Bible* did not teach that idea. Once a person has become a believer, they are part of the family of God. A believer is secure in their eternal destiny, even if that destiny is despite their own self. Simply because one is saved does not mean it is right to commit suicide; but Christ will not abandon anyone who believes—even when their faith may be shattered. Take refuge in this passage from 2 Timothy 2:13, *"If we are faithless, He remains faithful, for He cannot deny Himself."* Nothing can separate a person from God—not even the talking of one's life. According to Romans 8:38-39, Paul assured us, *"For I am convinced that neither death, nor life, nor angels, nor principalities, nor things present, nor things to come, nor powers, (39) nor height, nor depth, nor any other created thing, will be able to separate us from the love of God, which is in Christ Jesus our Lord."* God wanted people to know they are secure in their salvation, and all believers should take great comfort in that.

Our life on this earth is brief. That existence really is a mere breath as Job stated in Job 7:16, "I waste away; I will not live forever: leave me alone, for my days are but a breath." We are like grass—here today, gone tomorrow, like *The Bible* tells us in 1 Peter 1:24, *"For, 'ALL FLESH IS LIKE GRASS, AND ALL ITS GLORY LIKE THE FLOWER OF GRASS. THE GRASS WITHERS, AND THE FLOWER FALLS OFF.'"* We are the pride of God's creation as stated in Hebrews 2:7, *"'YOU HAVE MADE HIM FOR A LITTLE WHILE LOWER THAN THE ANGELS; YOU HAVE CROWNED HIM WITH GLORY AND HONOR, AND HAVE APPOINTED HIM OVER THE WORKS OF YOUR HANDS'"* It is wrong that human life seems so expendable here on this earth. There is so much premature death. Millions die of accidents, disease, wars, natural catastrophes and much more. That may not seem fair to you, and if it were not for the promise of Heaven, life may seem futile at best. The wisest man on earth wrote in Ecclesiastes 6:12, *"For who knows what is good for a man during his lifetime, during the few years of his futile life? He will spend them like a shadow. For who can tell a man what will be after him under the sun?"* God's ways are not our ways, and His thoughts are not our thoughts. He sees time differently than we do. We must accept those realities. The day will come, much sooner than we think, when God will reveal the mysteries of life, such as why things are the way they are, or why He allowed what He allowed. Then we will know, and it will all make sense. Until then, we must trust Him. I trust Him for my salvation and eternal destination, even though I do not know how to deal with what goes on down here at times.

We understand life is often not fair, but I will say one thing for Jesus Christ—He played fair. He did not lead a life of privilege. Jesus was born in a barn and grew up and worked as a blue collar worker. He was tempted. He went hungry. He was harassed, chased out of town, and was forever being threatened. During His public ministry, Jesus was homeless. He cried, laughed, and became angry. He suffered loneliness like few people will ever have to. There was no one the Son of God could talk to that would understand what He was going through and with what He was dealing. He did not complain, though. He did not consider equality with God a thing to be grasped. He stayed on message, and that message was the good news that God had indeed arrived. He loved the unlovable. He said what He meant, and meant what He said. He died a horrible and brutal death. Just think—we believers will see Jesus one day. We will meet him. We will be with our Friend. That is why Jesus came, and why He died the death He did. He had love and forgiveness for everyone who knew they needed it, and wanted it. Yes, He died for us alcoholics. We can trust the message from 1 Corinthians 6:9-11:

> *Or do you not know that the unrighteous will not inherit the kingdom of God? Do not be deceived; neither fornicators, nor idolaters, nor adulterers, nor effeminate, nor homosexuals, (10) nor thieves, nor the covetous, nor drunkards, nor revilers, nor swindlers, will inherit the kingdom of God. (11) Such were some of you; but you were washed, but you were sanctified, but you were justified in the name of the Lord Jesus Christ and in the Spirit of our God.*

This piece of Scripture settles that issue. We are forgiven; let no one ever tell you otherwise.

Lastly, I have a few words to direct to Satan at the end of this chapter. Satan, your destiny is sealed, and it is almost over for you now. Your reign on this earth is about to come to an abrupt halt. You are about to find out what jail and prison are really like, according to Revelation 20:2-3, "*And he laid hold of the dragon, the serpent of old, who is the devil and Satan, and bound him for a thousand years; (3) and he threw him into the abyss, and shut it and sealed it over him, so that he would not deceive the nations any longer, until the thousand years were completed;*

after these things he must be released for a short time." Satan, you are about to find out what it is like to be one of us. The reality of what you have been, and what you have done will fall down upon you. Do you realize how much carnage have you have caused or how many lives have you destroyed? God says you deserve the Lake of Fire in Revelation 20:10, *"And the devil who deceived them was thrown into the lake of fire and brimstone, where the beast and the false prophet are also; and they will be tormented day and night forever and ever."* All I know about you is what *The Bible* and Jesus taught about you. More times than I would ever want to admit, I went along with you, and for that I am undeniably sorry and broken; however, you will not have the final word. I say this with all my cynical heart, I will envy the angel who gets to throw your sorry, lying, miserable existence into that Lake of Fire!

Chapter 9

Let Me Count the Ways

A person can experience death in four main ways: physical death, mental death, emotional death, and spiritual death. I know of no other disease or illness that can kill a person more effectively in all four ways except for alcoholism or drug addiction. This addiction can kill one quickly, or it can produce a slow and painful death. More often than not though, alcoholism leads to a cruel and lonely death. Unlike many other types of diseases, alcoholism is seen as self-inflicted, and to a degree that is factual. What people need to realize however, is the alcoholic is not able to exercise the control over their drinking to point most people think they should be able. There is an intangible element that is almost impossible to explain. The medical profession refers to alcoholism as a disease because similar to cancer or any other disease, both the diagnosis and prognosis are fairly predictable for this problem. At times, alcoholics can no more control their addiction than a person can control the spread of their cancer.

We have all heard of alcoholics taking "the pledge," stating that they will stop drinking. The sad part is that they really meant it. They are completely serious and want it to stop, yet for that intangible reason, they cannot stop. It does not seem any one understands why they cannot stop. Just as the field of science has not found the answer for curing or preventing cancer and many other diseases, Science has not yet found that answer for alcoholism either. According to their website, the World Health Organization (WHO) has named alcoholism as the number one health threat worldwide, replacing the original threat from nicotine. That is a disease, my friend.

Alcoholism can physically kill a person in various ways. Liver, kidney and heart disease are just a few of the ways alcoholism physically attacks one's body. There are many types of accidents, including car accidents, which can occur and physically destroy people when the alcoholic is intoxicated. In its latter stages, alcoholism produces death in ways most people would never imagine. One result of alcoholism in its latter stages is malnutrition, since the alcoholic cannot eat anymore or hold anything down, their health is sorely compromised. More people die because of extreme alcohol consumption than people will ever be made aware. Family, friends, and loved ones may often cover up the actual cause of an alcoholic's death, but those individuals knew all too well the reason for that person's demise. Really though, what can those people say or do, or any one for that matter in such a situation? People may try to put the best perspective possible on the alcoholic's death, and attempt to explain the situation to the best of their ability, but to no avail. One reason the World Health Organization listed alcoholism as the number one health threat is that Science has recently discovered that alcohol does more damage to a human's vital organs than they had previously thought. Over time the effects of alcoholism can be physically devastating.

The second way one can die is mental death or by becoming what is known as brain dead. In this form of death, a person may physically still be alive or is being kept alive, but their brains are no longer functioning. In alcoholic circles this state is called "wet brain." If alcoholism's progress is allowed to run its full course, this demise is a genuine possibility. You can ask any health care professional, or go to any alcoholic treatment center to ask a few questions about alcoholism and this type of mental state. I warn you though that you may discover more than you ever wanted to know. For this mental death to occur, an alcoholic drinks enough alcohol effectively to render their brain inoperable. In essence, they kill it.

It is possible for people other than alcoholics to also die of this death. Some people may lapse into comas, never to return to active brain function again, because of some other disease or accident. In that state of inactive brain function, one's body may not be dead, but many people debate whether that person is really living since their brain simply will not function anymore. I personally would consider that stage a type of death. Laying there without any brain functionality would not be living to me. Some people may not subscribe to this perspective, especially if one believes life on this earth is all that exists.

The third form of death one can experience is an emotional death. You may see this casualty occur when a person has lost someone close, such as a spouse, after being together for many years. That individual may bereave the one who has passed away to such an extent they simply did not care to go on living anymore. Their loss just felt too painful to bear. I have known several people who have died in that manner. They simply shut down emotionally. You probably have heard someone say that someone died of a broken heart and I am confident that can happen. Most people who are reading this book probably know someone to whom this has happened since it is not uncommon.

Some people may question whether anyone ever wants to die. We can read in *The Bible* how Job wanted to die when he stated in Job 3:20-

21, *"Why is light given to him who suffers, and life to the bitter of soul, (21) who long for death, but there is none, and dig for it more than for hidden treasures."* One's life can emotionally get that difficult to endure. A person can suffer so much loss, whether it is people, relationships, finances, abilities or even one's dignity, that they are simply overwhelmed. Many alcoholics lose much, if not all of their dignity through their drinking and see no way to recapture it. David related to that condition in Psalm 44:15, when he stated, *"All day long my dishonor is before me and my humiliation has overwhelmed me."* When they reach that stage of humiliation or discouragement, the alcoholic can no longer mentally cope with their condition. They regret what has already happened, and fear the future even more, just as Job expressed in Job 3:25-26, *"For what I fear comes upon me, and what I dread befalls me. (26) I am not at ease, nor am I quiet, and I am not at rest, but turmoil comes."*

When the alcoholic reaches the point that he is that emotionally distraught, they might feel like suicide is a viable alternative. Again, Job even wished for death as an alternative to continuing to suffer as he stated in Job 7:15, *"So that my soul would choose suffocation; death rather than my pains."*

Alcoholics eventually find themselves in a place they *never* thought they would be—totally alone. The family, A.A. members and friends may have done all they could, but will almost always back away from the situation when the alcoholic degenerates. The Psalmist related to that condition when he said in Psalm 38:11, "*My loved ones and my friends stand aloof from my plague; and my kinsmen stand afar off.*" The alcoholic will come to a point where the result of their drinking will fall on them alone. At that stage, any relationship with wife, husband, boyfriend or girlfriend will have disappeared. David cried out in agony in Psalm 88:18, "*You have removed lover and friend far from me; my acquaintances are in darkness.*" At that point, the alcoholic cannot understand how life could have gotten away from them in such a manner. Even if they have been through treatment, exposed to A.A., have been warned in a thousand different ways, they still believed their current condition would not happen to them. Their past sufferings with alcohol did not even come to mind. That is the amnesia factor previously mentioned. The time about which the alcoholic was continually warned finally arrived. The alcoholic's emotional health will come into critical condition. They do not *want* to die, but in their current state living seems to be a worse alternative.

Normally when a person is about to die of some terrible condition, their family and friends are will gather with love and support. On the other hand, the alcoholic is more often not quite as fortunate. They isolate themselves, feeling instead that everyone has abandoned them—even God. David appeared to have felt that same emotion when he prayed in Psalm 39:12-13, *"Hear my prayer, O LORD, and give ear to my cry; do not be silent at my tears; for I am a stranger with You, a sojourner like all my fathers. (13) Turn Your gaze away from me, that I may smile again before I depart and am no more."*

I have come to that point myself where I feel I have experienced emotional death. I have no gas left in the tank. I cannot deal with the regrets of my past, much less deal with how I feel. I did not believe this state could ever happen to me. I never heard the bullet. Knowing all that I do about alcoholism, I should have, but I did not. As I mentioned before, I lived to satisfy my flesh, my addiction. I knew not to drink, but I still chose to drink. Drinking alcohol was all I knew, and as a result I killed myself. As Romans 7:9-10 so aptly describes, *"I was once alive apart from the Law; but when the commandment came, sin became alive and I died; (10) and this commandment, which was to result in life, proved to result in death for me."*

My commandment and law as an alcoholic were not to take that first drink. That idea may sound easy, but for me it was not. I felt I could always rely on alcohol to keep me going. Then the alcohol turned on me, like a good friend whom you could at one time trust. Through that deception, I have indeed discovered an important truth; alcoholism is not a state of mind, it is a power and a force. An alcoholic cannot even put up a good fight against alcoholism on their own strength. These two are a mismatch, even though at the time of his drinking the alcoholic will not see it that way.

Believe me, alcoholism is a complex disease. That is why A.A. teaches one must believe in a power greater than themselves to even have a chance to recover. Understanding this idea is the *only* thing that works. This leads me to my next point, which is very important for the reader to realize. You may ask how much of what has happened to me is the result of the disease of alcoholism, and how much of my situation is the result of my shortcomings as a human being. I have asked this question over and over. I have put this question to every expert in alcoholism that I can find, and I get the same answer—no one knows. That is that intangible aspect of alcoholism I alluded to earlier. I have read in a pamphlet about the topic of alcoholism that a seminar speaker once provided, that some scientists believe they are getting closer to isolating a gene that may cause certain people to become predisposed to addiction. Perhaps if they do, we can comprehend the reason the obsession can be so overwhelming at times, and scientists can also find a way to help treat or even remove that obsession. Unfortunately for now, this idea is only speculation. People can believe what they want, but the fact remains the alcoholic becomes a victim of a terrible and often misunderstood disease. Add to that fact the alcoholic is also still held responsible for all the consequences and ramifications of the disease, as though they had total control and should be able to somehow manage it. Without Divine intervention that control is just not going to happen. All of these points may not sound at all fair in my mind, but we know life is not always fair.

According to the WHO website, studies have shown alcoholics who are exposed to treatment and/or A.A. still have only a ten to twenty percent chance of reaching permanent sobriety. I am personally envious of that ten to twenty percent—very envious. I am saddened I had to learn about the real means of sobriety through failure. I do not believe I have ever learned any valuable lessons any other way. I do not say this fact to my credit. I had to discover these lessons by trial and error—a lot of error. My goal is that no one else has to find out these truths the same way. Many will tread that path of failure, as the studies show; but what a waste! It does not have to be that way. I would implore any practicing alcoholic or one considering relapse, to think before you take that first drink. You will not be any different from the millions of other people destroyed by alcoholism. You might *think* you will be different, but you won't be, and that is a fact. Live life the way it was intended—with a clear mind. Get any and all help that you need to stay sober. Do not let alcoholism win.

The fourth form of death I would like to discuss is a spiritual death. I have touched on this topic to some extent already, so I do not feel it necessary to further repeat that aspect in this chapter. I do want to remind you that we need to be able to live in the Spirit, and no one can successfully do that when they are drunk. Even though alcoholics look foolish and weak to the world, God sees those individuals struggling in another way. According to 1 Corinthians 1:27, *"but God has chosen the foolish things of the world to shame the wise, and God has chosen the weak things of the world to shame the things which are strong."* One must understand, however, neither God nor the Holy Spirit can effectively reach an alcoholic when they are drinking or when they are drunk. I am not talking about salvation here. I am talking about day-to-day life. When an alcoholic is actively engaged in drinking, that spiritual connection is severed. The last thing any alcoholic wants when they are drinking is a confrontation with God. Most alcoholics attempt to hide from God or dismiss Him completely. I believe that in both the preliminary as well as the intermediate stages of alcoholism, alcoholics can still hold on to their spiritual ties and beliefs. In the chronic stage of alcoholism though, I believe is all but impossible to stay connected spiritually with God, and that is oh, so dangerous. For all practical purposes, if a person does not fight the disease of alcoholism on a blatant spiritual level, sobriety becomes a mere dream, and eventually the alcoholic will reach the reasonable possibility of dying spiritually. The real misfortune is by that time, the alcoholic would likely never even know he has spiritually died. That is so sad. You may ask how that situation could occur. We can read in Titus 1:15, *"To the pure, all things are pure; but to those who are defiled and unbelieving, nothing is pure, but both their mind and their conscience are defiled."* Without a shadow of a doubt, sobriety is almost solely dependent on one's spiritual condition. I believe a person would do well never to forget that fact.

Chapter 10

More About Jesus

What I have written and said in this book, may not sit well with many people because it may seem too specific. Usually when a person mentions Jesus Christ and the A.A. program in the same breath, other people will often shudder at the idea. I believe this book has content that might make several people angry, and some people nervous. Jesus Christ always has that effect on people when His name is brought up. Jesus endured much persecution according to what *The Bible* says about Him. Jesus understood all too well His presence divided people. Christ even declared, "*Do not think that I came to bring peace on the earth; I did not come to bring peace, but a sword.*" Remember when Jesus went after the scribes and Pharisees in Matthew 23:13-36? He showed a side of God that should have put fear into anyone. He did not compromise. He did not mix His words. He did not display tolerance for self-righteous people.

People who did not believe or desire the truth stumbled over the teachings of Jesus. Peter said the same thing when he wrote in 1 Peter 2:7-8, *"This precious value, then, is for you who believe; but for those who disbelieve, 'THE STONE WHICH THE BUILDERS REJECTED, THIS BECAME THE VERY CORNER stone,' (8) and, "A STONE OF STUMBLING AND A ROCK OF OFFENSE'; for they stumble because they are disobedient to the word, and to this doom they were also appointed."*

Perhaps you have had the opportunity at some point to have a nice, philosophical discussion about God, religion, spiritual matters, or just life in general. The conversation may go along well and be a completely civil discussion until you mention the name of Jesus Christ. Suddenly the conversation becomes more personal. You are no longer using safe generalizations, and even the tone of the conversation changes. It is at that point a person will have to take a stand about what they believe. A person may choose simply to ignore Jesus Christ, believing all that they have heard about Him is untrue—as many people have chosen. *The Bible* even tells us this is a common perspective in 1 Corinthians 1:18, *"For the word of the cross is foolishness to those who are perishing, but to us who are being saved it is the power of God."*

If you do choose not to believe in Jesus Christ, and you do think and feel what you have heard is untrue, you had better hope that I am wrong about my convictions and belief in Jesus. When Christ related the example of the man who did not prepare for judgment in Luke 12:20, He stated, "*But God said to him, 'You fool! This very night your soul is required of you; and now who will own what you have prepared?'*" A person does not necessarily have to believe something is true for it to be so. Paul wrote in 1 Thessalonians 1:8-9, "*For the word of the Lord has sounded forth from you, not only in Macedonia and Achaia, but also in every place your faith toward God has gone forth, so that we have no need to say anything. (9) For they themselves report about us what kind of a reception we had with you, and how you turned to God from idols to serve a living and true God.*"

I added this additional chapter about Jesus in this book because I believed my view on Jesus may differ to some extent from many people. I think many people see Him as a ridged and stoic individual. Almost every movie that portrays Jesus and His life depicts Him in this manner. These movies show Him as a compassionate man, yet very proper and almost humorless. As I read the Gospels, I can see much more than that in Jesus' personality. I see how Jesus personally interacted with his disciples, or even the unique nicknames He gave some of them. These sections reveal something more. When Jesus was accused of hanging around the "less than stellar crowd of sinners," I discover even more about this man.

I think Jesus probably laughed a lot, and perhaps joked around. Since God created us with a sense of humor, as well as the ability to smile and laugh, it would seem only logical to conclude that Jesus exhibited these attributes. Despite the miracles He performed, Jesus drew immense crowds. I think people wanted to be near Him so badly, there had to be more to Him that people saw than just His abilities. There is still not a better feeling in the world than to smile and be able to laugh, and I am sure He was able to make people do both. I know He had a lighter side to Him. Although Jesus had the abilities of God, He was still completely human as well. He was very genuine.

I also believe the fact Jesus was loved by many different people apart from His disciples gives us further evidence of his genuine personality, since people generally do not love emotionless robots. Because people can see the human side of Christ and understand He truly was one of us, they can love Him even more. It is easy to love one of your own.

Even though Jesus never sinned, He did struggle with various people, places, and circumstances He encountered in much the same way we do. He cried. He became frightened and sometimes angry. I do not doubt Jesus was strict in many areas of His life, or that he displayed restraint, but He had a practical perspective of human nature. There can be no more evidence of that idea than His death on the cross. Jesus understood the frailty of human conduct *The Bible* had set, and He definitely understood our struggles with sin and ourselves. I have often wondered how Jesus felt when he became a human being after being God. That change must have been quite an experience for Him. We should all be grateful Jesus had that experience, for indeed, He has been one of us.

Because Jesus understands our needs so well, we should never forget He takes care of His own. He compares us to his own flock in John 10:14 when Christ stated, *"I am the good shepherd, and I know My own and My own know Me."*

I do not believe anyone can realize how great Jesus Christ was, not just as God, but as a human being. He not only talked the talk, but then He walked the walk. He did not live by the creed of "Do as I say, not as I do" as some people may. With all His gifts and abilities, He would not have had to play fair by experiencing the human condition so acutely, but He chose to still do so. Without a doubt, the most important thing Jesus wanted for this world, was that people believed He was and still is, God. In my opinion, if Jesus Christ was not God, then there is not one; however, I do believe Jesus is exactly Who He said He was.

Chapter 11

What's It All About?

Some of us may wonder about the big questions such as "What is life?" Perhaps you may have wondered what God's original intention was for all of us after He created us, or what our purpose may be. I believe God simply wanted friendship and companionship. Even though God provided total freedom of choice, He still wanted us to live within a framework He established to preserve the benefits of that life. He took the risk of love. God created us in such a way that He limited Himself on the control He could exercise on us and the decisions we would make. He refused to program us. I believe He regretted that decision. Genesis 6:6-7, stated that *"The LORD was sorry that He had made man on the earth, and He was grieved in His heart. (7) The LORD said, 'I will blot out man whom I have created from the face of the land, from man to animals to creeping things and to birds of the sky; for I am sorry that I have made them.'"* He allows us the free will to make choices that we might later regret. We cannot bring yesterday back or change it. If man had never chosen to disobey God, there also would have been no reason for His Son to die. God is omnipotent, which means He is all-knowing, but He gives us the chance to choose what is right, and He had to deal with the reality that man chose to defy Him. He took the risk to love us despite our sinful choices, but it still made Him sad we chose sin over His perfect plan for our lives. God wanted our love for Him to be genuine. For that to happen, God had to create us the way He did, and to give us *total* freedom of choice. He knew He would not turn back the clock, and I am sure He knew the risk He was taking. That is real love. I, for one, wish He would change yesterday and some of the bad decisions we make. I really do.

I want to explain something here that almost everyone tends to overlook, especially recovering alcoholics; God created this world with principles that are constant and reliable. We have fine examples of this idea in nature. For example, the sun rises in the East and sets in the West. The Earth orbits the Sun, thus night and day. Gravity and its influence on the tides are also an example of natural principles at work. My point is these natural principles are constant and reliable, and we cannot alter them. Applied spiritual principles are equally reliable. Natural principles treat all people the same, whether they are good or bad. There is no distinction. In comparison, a person who practices spiritual principles, even if they do not believe in God, still will reap the rewards and benefits of practicing those principles. That is why the Alcoholics Anonymous program works so well. Even though the leaders in those programs may not point directly or acknowledge the Biblical God, A.A. still uses His principles. The founders of A.A. discovered that important concept. They knew these principles worked and left the decision to believe in God up to the individual, just as God does. This is an example of the concept of attraction not promotion.

Unfortunately for alcoholics, there exists a grave danger I must warn you about; just because the spiritual principles work, does not mean you are eternally secure. You may be sober, but by ignoring Jesus Christ, you may have won an important battle, but you will lose the war—your eternity. Remember the chapter regarding the topic of Satan? Satan will allow a person to experience sobriety, if they in turn choose to give him their soul. This understanding has little to do with what you are, alcoholic, drug addict, or a friend or family member; but this situation refers to what and whom one believes. A person's drinking won't put them in Hell, and their sobriety alone will not put them in Heaven. If you are an alcoholic and drink, you may feel like you are experiencing Hell on earth—no doubt about that. Drinking will simply ruin your life, and you may very well not care what you believe any more. That is where the real danger lies.

I have heard on many occasions, people at an A.A. meeting say, "I will just stay sober and take my chances." With all the gambling I have done in my day, I have to tell you that is a bad bet! I strongly recommend to the person who may have said or thought that statement, that they take two hours out of their life and read the Gospel of John and the book of Romans from *The Bible*. If a person does that, I believe they may change that statement and belief. Getting drunk as an alcoholic is awful, but ignoring Jesus Christ is worse. Jesus never condoned sin, but He seemed to understand it; however, He never made allowances for unbelief. This is not intended to be a sermon, just facts you can discover for yourself from God's Word. Sin, by itself will never be able to cause one to go to Hell, but a person's unbelief in Jesus, and their willingness to ignore the price Christ paid for that sin, will.

I'd also suggest you read the first three of the Ten Commandments in Exodus 20:1-17. The Commandments are placed in order of their importance. While all the Commandments are equally valuable, it was no accident they were put in that order. Without those first three, there would be no need to be concerned with the other seven. The ability for a human being to want to live the last seven are directly related to their comprehension and belief of the first three. Often people fail to see the obvious ideas in front of them. I think Jesus Christ summed up all of life in one statement in Matthew 7:12, *"In everything, therefore, treat people the same way you want them to treat you, for this is the Law and the Prophets."* There it is. Believe in your Creator; put God first; and treat people the way you want them to treat you. That is what it is all about. In reality, that is all there is.

Chapter 12

Final Thoughts

I wrote this book for anyone who suffers from alcoholism and or drug addiction, but certainly with a bias toward Christians, as I tried to show with the cover of this book. This book was never intended to be about me personally, but about my beliefs pertaining to Christians, particularly about the disease of addiction—if one dares to call alcohol or drug addiction a disease. For the alcoholic, their addiction becomes more than a disease; it becomes that all-encompassing plague that in time destroys every aspect of the alcoholic's life—whether it's done quickly or over a longer period of time.

As discussed at length, this addiction physically, mentally, spiritually, and emotionally cripples and kills the addicted person. This disease must not be allowed to run its full course, for if it does, that person will inevitably experience a lonely, tragic, and premature death. That death may come in various ways, but it will definitely come if the drinking or drug using does not stop completely and forever. A person simply cannot manage or manipulate the disease of alcoholism. It must be arrested. I ask that you make no mistake about that fact, and never underestimate addiction the way I did. I beseech you to try to learn from the difficult lessons I learned and try to understand the message I am trying to convey. You can reach a point of no return with alcoholism. My mother was a prime example of someone who went through that situation. She smoked two to three packs of cigarettes a day all her adult life, and developed inoperable lung cancer. Even if she had quit smoking the day she found out, it would have made no difference. The damage had already been done, and she had already reached the point of no return. Alcoholism can produce the same result, only it has a more selective variety of ways from which to choose. I know of no other disease that can boast that level of destruction, but that is the sad reality of addiction. Even well-trained people in the field of addiction struggle fully to understand this concept, yet when an alcoholic reaches the chronic stage of alcoholism, the ability to choose to drink or not, is gone, never to return. At that point, only God and a spiritual change in a person's life can alter that condition, and that change is never accomplished by restoring that choice whether he is going to drink or not to the alcoholic. That change is produced by removing the obsession. Ask anyone in your church or A.A. who has been sober for years, and they will confirm this is they only way sobriety can occur. Sadly, at that stage, the odds of recovery are very slim. This book's purpose is to provide understanding about the true way an alcoholic will be able to stop drinking, before reaching that point.

During the early stages of alcoholism, the prognosis for an alcoholic to stop drinking with treatment and or A.A., with a spiritual awakening is possible, yet not probable. Although the chances are against it, many people do recover and arrest their addiction. I can assure you it can and does happen. As with any disease though, the earlier one catches the symptoms and treats the disease, the more probable it becomes for the alcoholic to cease drinking and recover. I cannot stress this point enough. As alcoholics go through the stages of alcoholism, they may at times fear they may die of sickness, accident, or any number of reasons. More often than not, once the alcohol reaches the chronic and final stages of alcoholism, they may not fear death any more at all. In fact, when facing the struggle of recovery, they may actually invite death.

As I had mentioned earlier, during the chronic stage of alcoholism, the alcoholic may constantly consider suicide, and at times, he may believe suicide is a viable alternative. I have personally experienced suicidal types of thoughts and behavior during that stage, and know many others have experienced the same. That is why it is so critical to diagnose alcoholism early, and then to understand what treatment will be needed. After one has diagnosed the alcoholic condition, they will have to commit to staying sober for the rest of their life, and not think of it as a stopgap measure. You cannot cut deals with addiction, attempting to manage or contain it. You can only arrest it one day at a time. I have heard people tell me that truth probably ten thousand times, and could never come to terms with that fact. My addiction blinded me. The addiction made me believe I could drink in moderation. In short, I was foolish to believe such a lie. I thought I knew better. I guess not. You can't be too dumb to recover, but you can think you're too smart to have to recover. I am a living testament to that fact.

I hope you will read this book, and think about its content. Your life and your eternal destiny are at stake. Alcoholism and addiction can destroy anyone—and I mean anyone—no matter what their station in life happens to be. Millions have already died of alcoholism, and like you, hoped they could change the way they dealt with their addiction, but could not. Do not simply read the stories of other alcoholics and wonder how the tragic results that happened to them could have happened. Instead, learn from them, and believe them to be true, because they are. Then be determined not to repeat their mistake. Trust first and foremost God, and second, trust the testimonials of recovering alcoholics who are willing to try to reach and teach you. Look around your circumstances, and realize the truth about your life. You do not have to understand everything I have explained, just believe it. I cannot tell you how badly I wish I would have made that decision earlier. I really can't. I would give my life for a chance to turn back the hands of time, and the opportunity to rectify poor choices, but God will not change yesterday for me or for anyone else. If you apply what I have written in this book to your life, you will likely never want to risk your life or your soul at the expense of your addiction. That, my friend, is the whole idea.

Live life the way it was intended to be lived—with a clear and sober mind. If you do, you will live a free life, and not be a poor and disillusioned slave to your addiction. May God impress on you what He wanted to impress on me. Let Him, and may God bless all your efforts.

www.ingramcontent.com/pod-product-compliance
Lightning Source LLC
Chambersburg PA
CBHW031652040426
42453CB00006B/279